PASTA
Cook Book

PAULO EPISCOPO

D1189125

MEREHURST

Published in 1995 by Merehurst Limited
Ferry House, 51–57 Lacy Road, Putney, London SW15 1PR

Reprinted 1996

Copyright © 1995 Merehurst Limited

ISBN 1–85391–563–3

A catalogue record for this book is available from the
British Library

Series Editor: Valerie Barrett
Design: Clive Dorman
Illustrations: Keith Sparrow

Typeset by Clive Dorman & Co.
Colour Separation by P&W Graphics Pty Ltd, Singapore
Printed and bound in Great Britain by
Mackays of Chatham PLC, Chatham, Kent

RECIPE NOTES

 Indicates dishes that cook in under 35 minutes

● Follow one set of measurements only, do not mix metric and imperial

● All spoon measures are level

● Always taste and adjust seasonings to suit your own preferences

 Indicates dishes that are suitable for vegetarians

CONTENTS

INTRODUCTION

When you think of pasta, you think of Italy, and although it is true that the Italians have perfected the art of pasta-making, its actual origins are lost in antiquity. Some form of pasta, that is a boiled dough of flour and water, was a staple food for many early civilisations. It was probably an early cook experimenting after the discovery of flour! Pasta was around in China over 6000 years ago. Museum records show that ravioli and noodles were being eaten in Rome in 1284. Some years before Marco Polo returned from China, and supposedly introduced pasta to Italy.

The early pastas were baked first and then often served with sugar and honey. Over the centuries pasta developed into different shapes and sizes and was cooked in liquid, such as soups, and then with sauces. Stuffed pastas appeared in the Middle Ages. The thing that really changed the way pasta was eaten was the introduction of the tomato to Italy in the sixteenth century. Originally from Mexico and Peru, the tomato was at first regarded with suspicion by Italians. However, the tomato adapted well to the climate and soil, and found a home in Naples. From then on the tomato and pasta became virtually inseparable, and pasta became almost totally a savoury dish.

Today pasta is one of the most easily prepared, versatile and filling ingredients you can buy. We know now what was probably always taken for granted, that pasta is very good for us. It is high in protein, low in sodium and fat, contains vitamins, iron, minerals, fibre and uses no preservatives. Whether it is simply boiled and served with a splash of oilve oil and garlic, or formed into a more intricate baked dish, it is never boring.

TYPES OF PASTA

Convenience of handling and storing, texture and flavour, and good cooking properties all contribute to the type of pasta that you choose to buy and use. Some people swear by fresh pasta whilst others prefer the convenience and texture of dried. Experiment by trying different types and decide for yourself.

Packaged Dried Pasta

It is made from durum wheat semolina and water and some-times labelled 'pasta di semolina di grana duro'. Eggs are some-times used in the pasta and this may be marked on the packet as 'all'uovo'. As dried pasta requires rehydration as well as cooking, it takes longer to cook than the fresh variety. Dried pasta makes a good store cupboard standby as it keeps for a long time.

Commercial Fresh Pasta

Fresh pasta is soft and pliable and may be sold loose or in plastic packs. It is made from durum wheat semolina and egg. Being fresh, it cooks in just a few minutes. Although fresh pasta keeps for only a few days, it freezes well and can be kept frozen for several months. To freeze, divide into serving portions, place in freezer bags, seal, label and freeze. If purchased in a plastic pack, simply place in the freezer as it is.

HOW MUCH PASTA TO SERVE

Pasta type	First course per serving	Main meal per serving
Dried	60-75g (2-2½ oz)	75-100g (2½-3½ oz)
Fresh	75-100g (2½-3½ oz)	125-150g (4-5 oz)
Filled pasta such as ravioli	150-180g (5-6 oz)	180-200g (6-7 oz)

COOKING PASTA

Cook pasta in a large, deep saucepan of water. The general rule is 1 litre (1¾ pints) water to 100g (3½ oz) pasta. Bring water to a rolling boil, toss in salt to taste – in Italy 1 tablespoon per 100g (3½ oz) is usual – then stir in pasta. If you wish, add a tablespoon of oil. When the water comes back to the boil, begin timing. The pasta is done when it is 'al dente', that is tender but with resistance to the bite. Remove the pasta from the water by straining through a colander or lifting out of the saucepan with tongs or large fork. Never rinse pasta unless it is to be used for a salad, when it is cooled rapidly by rinsing under cold water. The hot drained pasta is now ready for the sauce. Stir through a little oil or melted butter and serve topped with sauce, or toss pasta straight into the sauce and mix together.

KNOW YOUR PASTA

Pasta comes in an array of shapes and sizes, which can some-times be confusing. However, many shapes are interchange-able and it is great fun to invent your own combinations of pasta and sauce. There are some tips that will help you when deciding which shapes to use. Thin, long pasta needs a good clinging sauce; hollow or twisted shapes take chunky sauces; wide, flat noodles need rich sauces; and delicate shapes require a light sauce without large pieces in it.

Angel's hair pasta Also labelled as 'capelli di angelo', this is an extremely long thin pasta that is dried in coils to prevent it from breaking. Because it is so delicate, always serve with a light sauce.

Cannelloni This large hollow pasta is most often stuffed, topped with a sauce and cheese and then baked. Cannelloni can also be boiled and then stuffed and deep-fried. Lasagne sheets are also often used for baked cannelloni. The filling is spread down the centre of the pasta before rolling up.

Farfalle Meaning 'butterflies' this is a bow shaped pasta. There is another bow shaped pasta called fiochetti. Both are ideal for serving with meat and vegetable sauces as the sauce becomes trapped in the folds.

Fettucine A flat ribbon pasta that is used in a similar way to spaghetti. Often sold coiled in nests, fettucine is particularly good with creamy sauces which cling better than heavier ones.

Lasagne These flat sheets of pasta are most often layered with a meat, fish or vegetable sauce, topped with cheese, then baked. Instant or oven-ready lasagne that does not require precooking is also available. Lasagnette are long flat ribbons of lasagne with a ruffled edge.

Linguine This long thin pasta looks somewhat like spaghetti but is in fact thin narrow ribbons. It can be used in the same way as spaghetti, fettucine and tagliatelle.

Macaroni This is a generic term applying to a number of hollow shapes. Short-cut or elbow macaroni, very common outside of Italy, is most often used in baked dishes and in the ever-popular Macaroni Cheese.

Orecchiette Small ear shaped pasta.

Pappardelle This is a very wide ribbon pasta which was tradi-tionally served with a sauce made of hare, herbs and wine. It goes well with any rich sauce.

Pastina There are numerous small pasta, such as anellini (rings), ditalini (tiny tubes), stellini (stars), puntette (rice shapes) and alphabets. They are mostly added to soups.

Penne A short tubular pasta, similar to macaroni, but with ends cut at an angle rather than straight. It is particularly suited to being served with meat and heavier sauces, which catch in the hollows.

Rigatoni The ridges of this macaroni help sauces to cling to it. Available in many different types it is most often used in baked dishes. Larger rigatoni can also be stuffed and baked.

Rotelli This wheel shaped pasta is useful in savoury baked dishes, salads and soups.

Shell pasta Also called conchiglie, if large, or conchigliette if smaller. The large shells are ideal for stuffing and a fish filling is often favoured because of the shape of the pasta. Small shells are popular in casseroles, soups and salads.

Spaghetti Deriving its name from the Italian word 'spago' meaning string, spaghetti is the most popular and best known of all pastas outside of Italy. It can be simply served with butter or oil and is good with almost any sauce.

Spaghettini This is very thin spaghetti (also known as fedelini) and is traditionally served with fish and shellfish sauces.

Spiral pasta Also called fusilli or spirelli these are spiral or corkscrew shapes which are great with meat sauces as the sauce becomes trapped in the coils or twists.

Tagliarini Similar to fettucine, this is the name often given to homemade fettucine.

Tagliatelle Another of the flat ribbon pastas, it is used in the same ways as fettucine.

Vermicelli This is what the Neapolitans call spaghetti. It comes in many varieties, with very thin vermicelli being sold in clusters, and is ideal for serving with very light sauces. The longer, thicker vermicelli is served in the same way as spaghetti.

Filled Pasta:
Agnolotti half-moon shaped
Cappelletti hat shaped
Ravioli squares
Tortellini crescents folded to form a hole in the middle

HOMEMADE PASTA

A general rule to follow when making pasta is ; 1 large egg to every 100g (3½ oz) flour, and 100g (3½ oz) flour per person for a main course serving.

BASIC PASTA DOUGH

4 large eggs
400g (16 oz) flour
large pinch salt
a little water

1 Place eggs in a large bowl and whisk to combine. Sift flour and salt into egg mixture.

2 Using a fork first and then your hands, mix the eggs into the flour to form a coarse dough. Add a little flour or water if necessary.

3 Turn dough onto a lightly floured surface and knead by hand for 6-8 minutes or until a smooth elastic dough is formed. The dough can also be kneaded in a food processor for 2-3 minutes. Cover dough with a cloth and set aside to rest at room temperature for 15 minutes. Divide dough into manageable pieces and roll out either by hand or using a pasta machine and then use as required.

Homemade pasta must be eaten fresh. It does not dry successfully, as the high moisture content makes the pasta dry out too quickly and it cracks.

FLAVOURED PASTA

Many ingredients can be added to pasta to give colour and flavour. As many of these additives contain liquid or have 'short' qualities, the dough may be harder to work once you begin kneading. A little extra flour or water, as necessary, will adjust the balance.

Tomato Pasta

Beat 2½ tablespoons tomato purée into the eggs, then follow the method as for Homemade Pasta.

Spinach Pasta

Cook 75g (2½ oz) spinach, then drain thoroughly and squeeze to remove as much moisture as possible. Purée spinach with a pinch of nutmeg, then combine with the eggs and follow method as for Homemade Pasta.

Wholemeal Pasta
Use half white flour and half wholemeal flour. Follow method as for making Homemade Pasta.

Chocolate Pasta
Beat 1 tablespoon cocoa powder into the eggs, then follow method for Homemade Pasta.

ROLLING PASTA BY HAND

If you are going to roll pasta by hand you will need a large rolling pin and work surface. Lightly flour the work surface, then, using your hands, press the dough flat and roll it out, maintaining a circular shape. Keep rolling until the dough is a large thin sheet that is almost transparent. As you roll the dough, let some of it hang over the edge of the work surface - this helps to stretch it.

CUTTING PASTA BY HAND

Always use a large sharp knife when cutting pasta by hand.

Tagliatelle
Roll pasta dough to 3-5 mm (⅛-¼ inch) thickness and cut into very wide strips. Roll strips up loosely to form a cylinder and cut into even widths. Shake out pasta into loose 'nests'.

Lasagne and Cannelloni
Roll pasta dough to 3-5 mm (⅛-¼ inch) thickness. For lasagne sheets, cut pasta to whatever size will fit your dish. A convenient size is 10 x 12 cm (4 x 5 inch). For cannelloni, cut pasta into 10 x 12 cm (4 x 5 inch). The cannelloni can then be cooked, filled with a stuffing and rolled up before baking.

Pappardelle and Farfalle
Roll pasta dough to 3-5 mm (⅛-¼ inch) thickness. To make pappardelle, using a zigzag pastry wheel, cut dough strips 2 cm (¾ inch) wide and 30 cm (12 inches) long. For farfalle, using a pastry wheel, cut pasta into 5 cm (2 inch) squares, then pinch together the middle of each square to give a bow effect.

USING A PASTA MACHINE

Make the dough and divide into manageable pieces (a good rule is to divide into the same number of pieces as there were eggs in the dough). Set the rollers of the pasta machine on the widest setting and feed the dough through. Fold the rolled dough into quarters to make a square.

Feed the dough through the machine again, then fold again. Repeat folding and rolling of dough 4-5 times or until you have a shiny, smooth and elastic dough. Close the rollers a notch at a time and roll the dough thinner and thinner until the desired thickness is reached.

If making lasagne or filled pasta, use the pasta immediately. Otherwise, to cut the pasta, leave to dry for 10 minutes and then feed each strip through the appropriate blades. As the cut strips of dough emerge from the machine catch them on your hand. Place them on a clean cloth and set aside to dry at room temperature for about 30 minutes or until dough is dry enough to prevent sticking, but is not brittle.

MAKING FILLED PASTA

Make the pasta as described and use as soon as it is made to avoid drying out. For this reason it is important to have the filling ready and waiting.

Using a Mould

There are trays available that come in a selection of pre-pressed ravioli shapes, accompanied by a little rolling pin. These moulds give a ravioli of uniform shape and size.

Making a Filled Sheet of Ravioli

On a lightly floured surface, roll pasta dough out to 2 mm (1/16 inch) thickness and cut into strips. Place strips on a tea towel or floured surface and cover with a damp cloth. Keep unused dough covered.

Place small mounds of filling at 4 cm (1½ inch) intervals along a strip of dough. Then lay a second strip over the top.

Press dough down firmly between the mounds of filling to join the pasta. Using a pastry wheel, cut the ravioli. Place prepared ravioli on a tea towel to dry for 30 minutes. Cook in boiling water for about 4 minutes.

Half-moon ravioli can be made by cutting the pasta dough

into 5 cm (2 inch) circles. A small amount of filling is then placed in the middle of the circle. The circle is folded over and the edges pressed firmly together. Dry and cook as for ravioli.

Making Tortellini

Cut 5 cm (2 inch) circles of pasta dough. Place a small amount of filling slightly to one side of the middle. Fold over circle so that it falls just short of the other side. Press edges firmly together, curve the semi-circle round, then pinch the edges together. Dry and cook as for ravioli.

Making Capelletti

Cut 5 cm (2 inch) squares of pasta. Place a small amount of filling in the centre of each square, then fold in half diagonally to form a triangle, leaving a slight overlap between the edges. Press firmly to seal. Wrap the long side of the triangle round a finger until the two ends overlap. Press ends together with the point of the triangle upright. Dry and cook as for ravioli.

SOUPS

There are always odds and ends of pasta left in the cupboard and a good way to use them up is to add them to soup. Pasta soups are easy to make and they are often filling enough to be served as a meal with some crusty bread. Smaller pasta shapes are best in soups, but you can always break spaghetti or ribbon noodles into small pieces and use these as well.

HEARTY MACARONI SOUP

E A S Y !

This hearty soup of vegetables, pasta, beans and tofu, makes a substantial one-dish meal. While the recipe uses macaroni you can in fact use any pasta you wish.

Serves 4

2 teaspoons vegetable oil
1 red onion, chopped
2 fresh red chillies, de-seeded and finely chopped
1 red pepper, chopped
2 carrots, chopped
2 courgettes, sliced
1 litre (1¾ pints) vegetable stock
400g (14 oz) canned tomatoes, undrained and mashed
250g (8 oz) elbow macaroni
400g (14 oz) canned red kidney beans, rinsed
1 tablespoon finely chopped fresh thyme or ½ teaspoon dried thyme
200g (7 oz) firm tofu, chopped
freshly ground black pepper

1 Heat oil in a large saucepan over a medium heat. Add onion and chillies and cook, stirring, for 3 minutes or until onion is soft.

2 Add red pepper, carrots, courgettes, stock, tomatoes and macaroni, bring to a gentle boil and simmer for 10 minutes or until macaroni is cooked.

3 Stir in beans, thyme and tofu, bring to a gentle boil and simmer for 2 minutes or until heated through. Season to taste with black pepper.

ITALIAN CHICKEN SOUP

EASY!

A clear chicken broth made with fresh chicken and vegetables which makes a nutritious and delicious light meal that any weight-watcher will love.

Serves 6

1.7 litres (3 pints) chicken stock
4 chicken breast fillets, skinned
1 teaspoon whole black peppercorns
4 bay leaves
1 sprig fresh rosemary
1 onion, chopped
1 red pepper, chopped
2 carrots, chopped
180g (6 oz) short pasta shapes, such as macaroni
250g (8 oz) cabbage, shredded
2 tablespoons grated Parmesan cheese

1 Place stock in a large saucepan and bring to the boil. Add chicken breasts, peppercorns, bay leaves and rosemary. Reduce heat, cover and simmer for 20 minutes or until chicken is just cooked.

2 Using a slotted spoon, remove chicken from pan and set aside to drain. Strain stock and return liquid to a clean saucepan. Add onion, red pepper, carrots and pasta to stock, cover, then bring to a gentle boil and simmer for 20 minutes or until pasta is cooked and vegetables are tender.

3 Slice chicken. Stir chicken and cabbage into soup and cook for 5 minutes longer. Just prior to serving, stir in Parmesan cheese.

SPAGHETTI BASIL SOUP

REALLY EASY!

A quickly made soup of spaghetti, almonds, onions and basil. Sprinkled with Parmesan cheese and served with bread rolls, this soup makes a wonderful summer lunch dish.

Serves 4

150g (5 oz) spaghetti, broken into pieces
2 tablespoons vegetable oil
1 onion, chopped
2 cloves garlic, crushed
60g (2 oz) slivered almonds
1 litre (1¾ pints) chicken stock
30g (1 oz) shredded fresh basil leaves
freshly ground black pepper

1 Cook spaghetti in boiling water in a large saucepan following packet directions. Drain and set aside.

2 Heat oil in a large saucepan and cook onion, garlic and almonds, stirring over a medium heat for 6-7 minutes or until onions are transparent.

3 Add stock and basil to pan and bring to the boil, reduce heat, cover and simmer for 10 minutes. Stir in spaghetti and season to taste with black pepper. Spoon soup into bowls and serve immediately.

MINESTRONE

EASY!

This traditional soup of beans, mixed vegetables and pasta is a meal in itself.

Serves 6 as a main meal
300g (10 oz) dried white haricot beans
1.5 litres (2½ pints) water
1.5 litres (2½ pints) chicken stock
125g (4 oz) mushrooms, sliced
150g (5 oz) green beans, chopped
2 carrots, chopped
2 courgettes, sliced
1 leek, sliced
150g (5 oz) small shell pasta
400g (14 oz) canned tomatoes, undrained and mashed
freshly ground black pepper
grated Parmesan cheese

1 Place dried beans and I litre (1¾ pints) water in a large bowl, cover and set aside to soak for 8 hours or overnight.

2 Drain beans and rinse in cold water. Place beans and stock in a large saucepan, bring to the boil and boil rapidly for 10 minutes. Reduce heat, cover and simmer for 1 hour or until beans are tender.

3 Add mushrooms, green beans, carrots, courgettes, leek and remaining 500 ml (16 fl oz) water to pan. Bring to the boil, then reduce heat, cover and simmer for 30 minutes. Stir pasta and tomatoes into soup and cook for 10 minutes longer or until pasta is tender. Season to taste with black pepper. Sprinkle with Parmesan cheese and serve immediately.

SPINACH SOUP

REALLY EASY!

A very quick tasty soup made with chicken stock, pasta shapes and spinach, thickened with egg yolks.

Serves 6

1 litre (1¾ pints) chicken stock
60g (2 oz) small pasta shapes
250g (8oz) frozen chopped spinach, thawed
freshly ground black pepper,
2 egg yolks

1 Place stock in a large saucepan and bring to the boil. Add pasta and spinach and cook, stirring occasionally, for 10 minutes or until pasta is tender. Season to taste with black pepper.

2 Place egg yolks in a small bowl and whisk to combine. Whisk a little hot soup into egg yolks, then stir egg yolk mixture into soup. Serve immediately.

MINESTRONE • SPINACH SOUP

VERMICELLI ONION SOUP

REALLY EASY!

A creamy soup with chicken stock, onions and vermicelli.

Serves 6

60g (2 oz) butter
3 onions, thinly sliced
1 tablespoon flour
300ml (10 fl oz) hot chicken stock
1 litre (1¾ pints) milk
60g (2 oz) vermicelli, broken into pieces
freshly ground black pepper

1 Melt butter in a large saucepan and cook onions, stirring, over a medium heat for 6-7 minutes or until soft. Stir in flour, then gradually stir in hot stock. Cook, stirring constantly, for 4-5 minutes or until soup is smooth and thickened.

2 Stir in milk and bring to the boil. Add vermicelli and season to taste with black pepper. Cook, stirring frequently, for 8-10 minutes or until vermicelli is tender.

ITALIAN BEAN SOUP

REALLY EASY!

Thick soups such as this, made with pulses and pasta, are excellent for filling hungry teenagers.

Serves 6

1 tablespoon olive oil
2 onions, chopped
2 cloves garlic, crushed
1 red pepper, chopped
1.5 litres (2½ pints) chicken or vegetable stock
125g (4 oz) small pasta shapes
125 ml (4 fl oz) red wine
400g (14 oz) canned tomatoes, undrained and mashed
2 tablespoons tomato purée
300g (10 oz) canned red kidney beans, drained
freshly ground black pepper

1 Heat oil in a large saucepan and cook onions, garlic and red pepper for 4-5 minutes or until onion softens.

2 Stir in stock, pasta, wine, tomatoes, tomato purée and beans. Bring to the boil, then reduce heat and simmer for 15 minutes. Season to taste with black pepper.

STARTERS

A light and appetising pasta dish makes an excellent first course. Be careful not to serve too large a portion or you will be too full to eat the rest of the meal. About 60g (2 oz) per person is enough. These recipes also make very good light meals if served with a salad and some fresh crusty bread.

PASTA WITH FRESH THYME

R E A L L Y   E A S Y !

To make shavings of Parmesan cheese you will need a piece of fresh Parmesan cheese. Use a vegetable peeler or a coarse grater to remove shavings of cheese.

Serves 6

500g (1 lb) fresh herb pasta or plain pasta of your choice
freshly ground black pepper
fresh Parmesan cheese

Thyme Sauce
60g (2 oz) butter
90 ml (3 fl oz) white wine vinegar
3 tablespoons roughly chopped fresh thyme

1 Cook pasta in boiling water in a large saucepan, following packet directions. Drain, set aside and keep warm.

2 To make sauce, melt butter in a small saucepan and add vinegar and thyme. Bring to a gentle boil and simmer over a low heat, stirring, for 4 minutes,

3 Spoon sauce over pasta and toss to combine. Season to taste with black pepper and top with shavings of Parmesan cheese.

PASTA WITH ROASTED GARLIC AND TOMATOES

$\boxed{V}$

EASY!

Fresh fettuccine topped with oven roasted tomatoes and garlic and Mint Pesto. When garlic is roasted it looses its pungent strong taste and odour and becomes sweet and subtle.

Serves 8

2 tablespoons olive oil
16 plum tomatoes, quartered
32 cloves garlic, unpeeled
sea salt
500g (1 lb) fresh fettuccine

Mint Pesto

1 large bunch fresh mint
4 tablespoons fresh grated Parmesan cheese
1 clove garlic, crushed
3 tablespoons pine kernels
3 tablespoons olive oil

1 Preheat oven to 180C,350F,Gas 4. Place oil, tomatoes and garlic in a large baking dish. Toss to coat and sprinkle with sea salt. Bake for 35 minutes or until garlic is deep brown in colour. Keep warm.

2 To make pesto, place mint leaves, Parmesan cheese, garlic and pine kernels in a food processor or blender and process until finely chopped. With machine running, gradually add oil and continue processing until a thick paste forms.

3 Cook pasta in boiling water in a large saucepan, following packet directions. Drain and keep warm.

4 Just prior to serving, remove skin from garlic cloves. To serve, divide hot pasta between serving plates, then top with some of the roasted tomatoes and roasted garlic and a spoonful of Mint Pesto.

TAGLIATELLE WITH PISTACHIOS

REALLY EASY!

Noodles tossed with pistachio nuts, basil, cherry tomatoes and green peppercorns.

Serves 6

500g (1 lb) fresh spinach tagliatelle
45g (1½ oz) butter
60g (2 oz) pistachio nuts, shelled
4 tablespoons shredded fresh basil leaves
250g (8 oz) cherry tomatoes, halved
1 tablespoon green peppercorns in brine, drained

1 Cook tagliatelle in boiling water in a large saucepan, following packet directions. Drain, set aside and keep warm.

2 Melt butter in a frying pan, add pistachio nuts, basil, tomatoes and green peppercorns. Cook over a medium heat, stirring constantly, for 4-5 minutes or until heated through. Toss tomato mixture with pasta and serve.

SPAGHETTI AND PESTO

REALLY EASY!

Pesto is also good with ribbon pasta such as tagliatelle or fettuccine.

Serves 6
500g (1 lb) spaghetti

Pesto
125g (4 oz) fresh basil leaves
3 tablespoons pine kernels
4 cloves garlic, crushed
4 tablespoons olive oil
freshly ground black pepper

1 Cook spaghetti in boiling water in a large saucepan, following packet directions. Drain, set aside and keep warm.

2 To make Pesto, place basil, pine kernels and garlic in a food processor or blender and process to finely chop all ingredients. With machine running, add oil in a steady steam. Season to taste with black pepper.

3 Add Pesto to spaghetti and toss to combine. Serve immediately.

PENNE WITH SAFFRON AND PRAWNS

REALLY EASY!

Pasta with prawns and mangetout tossed in a saffron sauce. Food flavoured with saffron has a distinctive aroma, a bitter honey-like taste and a strong yellow colour.

Serves 6
500g (1 lb) penne
500g (1 lb) cooked prawns, peeled and deveined
125g (4 oz) mangetout, blanched

Saffron Sauce
30g (1 oz) butter
1 tablespoon flour
250 ml (8 fl oz) milk
½ teaspoon saffron threads or pinch saffron powder
1 tablespoon chopped fresh sage or ½ teaspoon dried sage

1 Cook pasta in boiling water in a large saucepan, following packet directions. Drain, set aside and keep warm.

2 To make sauce, melt butter in a small saucepan over a medium heat, stir in flour and cook for 1 minute. Remove pan from heat and whisk in milk, saffron and sage. Return pan to heat and cook, stirring, for 3-4 minutes or until sauce boils and thickens.

3 Add prawns and mangetout to hot pasta and toss to combine. Top with sauce and serve immediately.

PASTA WITH FRESH TOMATO SAUCE

R E A L L Y   E A S Y !

Fine pasta topped with a tomato sauce and garnished with rocket and Parmesan

Serves 6
500g (1 lb) angel's hair pasta or fine spaghetti
30g (1 oz) grated Parmesan cheese
125g (4 oz) rocket or watercress, trimmed
fresh Parmesan cheese

Fresh Tomato Sauce
4 ripe large tomatoes, skinned and chopped
60 ml (2 fl oz) vegetable stock
1 tablespoon balsamic or red wine vinegar
freshly ground black pepper

1 Cook pasta in boiling water in a large saucepan, following packet directions. Drain, set aside and keep warm.

2 To make sauce, place tomatoes in a food processor or blender and process until smooth. With machine running, add stock, vinegar and black pepper to taste and process to combine.

3 Add grated Parmesan cheese to hot pasta and toss to combine. To serve, top pasta with sauce, rocket leaves and shavings of Parmesan cheese.

PENNE WITH SAFFRON & PRAWNS • PASTA WITH FRESH TOMATO SAUCE

FETTUCCINE WITH SPINACH SAUCE

REALLY EASY!

Plain pasta ribbons lightly speckled with a creamy spinach and cheese sauce

Serves 6
500g (1 lb) plain fettuccine
fresh Parmesan cheese

Spinach Sauce
15g (½ oz) butter
1 clove garlic, crushed
1 leek, sliced
500g (1 lb) young spinach, chopped
250g (8 oz) reduced-fat cream cheese
2 tablespoons grated Parmesan cheese
125 ml (4 fl oz) chicken stock

1 Cook pasta in boiling water in a large saucepan, following packet directions. Drain, set aside and keep warm.

2 To make sauce, melt butter in a saucepan over a medium heat, add garlic and leek and cook, stirring, for 3 minutes. Add spinach and cook for 3 minutes longer or until spinach wilts.

3 Place spinach mixture, cream cheese, grated Parmesan cheese and stock in a food processor or blender and process until smooth. Return sauce to a clean saucepan, bring to a gentle boil and simmer, stirring constantly, for 5-6 minutes or until sauce thickens and is heated through.

4 Spoon sauce over hot pasta and toss to combine. Serve topped with shavings of Parmesan cheese.

LINGUINE WITH CHILLI AND LEMON

REALLY EASY!

Fresh pasta cooked and tossed with garlic, chillies, rocket, lemon and Parmesan.

Serves 6

500g (1 lb) fresh linguine or spaghetti
2 tablespoons olive oil
6 cloves garlic, peeled
2 fresh red chillies, de-seeded and sliced
125g (4 oz) rocket or watercress, shredded
1 tablespoon finely grated lemon rind
2 tablespoons lemon juice
freshly ground black pepper
90g (3 oz) grated Parmesan cheese

1 Cook pasta in boiling water in a large saucepan, following packet directions. Drain, set aside and keep warm.

2 Heat oil in a frying pan over a low heat, add garlic and chillies and cook, stirring, for 6 minutes or until garlic is golden. Add garlic mixture, rocket, lemon rind, lemon juice, black pepper to taste and Parmesan cheese to hot pasta and toss to combine.

FETTUCCINE WITH SPINACH SAUCE • LINGUINE WITH CHILLI & LEMON

TAGLIATELLE WITH CHILLI OCTOPUS

EASY!

Baby octopus flavoured with a Chilli Ginger Marinade, mixed with Tomato Sauce and served on a bed of pasta. Substitute squid rings for octopus if you prefer.

Serves 6
1 kg (2 lb) baby octopus, cleaned
500g (1 lb) spinach tagliatelle

Chilli Ginger Marinade
1 tablespoon sesame oil
1 tablespoon grated fresh ginger
2 tablespoons lime juice
2 tablespoons sweet chilli sauce

Tomato Sauce
2 teaspoons vegetable oil
3 spring onions, sliced diagonally
400g (14 oz) tomato passata

1 To make marinade, place sesame oil, ginger, lime juice and chilli sauce in a large bowl and mix to combine. Add octopus, toss to coat, cover and marinate in the refrigerator for 3-4 hours.

2 Cook pasta in boiling water in a large saucepan, following packet directions. Drain, set aside and keep warm.

3 To make sauce, heat oil in a saucepan over a medium heat. Add spring onions and cook, stirring, for 1 minute. Stir in tomato passata, bring to a gentle boil and simmer for 4 minutes.

4 Cook octopus under a preheated hot grill for 5-7 minutes or until tender. Add octopus to sauce and toss to combine. Spoon octopus mixture over hot pasta and toss.

FETTUCCINE ALFREDO

REALLY EASY!

A very simple dish of pasta with butter and Parmesan cheese.

Serves 6

500g (1 lb) fettuccine
150g (5 oz) butter, chopped and softened
125g (4 oz) grated fresh Parmesan cheese
freshly ground black pepper

1 Cook pasta in boiling water in a large saucepan, following packet directions. Drain well and place in a large serving bowl.

2 Scatter butter and Parmesan cheese over the hot pasta, season to taste with black pepper, toss and serve immediately.

PASTA WITH SIX HERB SAUCE

REALLY EASY!

Equally delicious as a light meal or the first course of a dinner party, this dish must be made using fresh not dried herbs. However, the herbs can be changed according to what is available. If you can only get four of the herbs then just use those.

Serves 6 as a starter, 4 as a light meal
500g (1 lb) pasta shapes of your choice

Six Herb Sauce
30g (1 oz) butter
2 tablespoons chopped fresh rosemary
12 small fresh sage leaves
12 small fresh basil leaves
2 tablespoons fresh marjoram leaves
2 tablespoons fresh oregano leaves
2 tablespoons chopped fresh parsley
2 cloves garlic, chopped
60 ml (2 fl oz) white wine
60 ml (2 fl oz) vegetable stock

1 Cook pasta in boiling water in a large saucepan, following packet directions. Drain, set aside and keep warm.

2 To make sauce, melt butter in a saucepan over a medium heat. Add rosemary, sage, basil, marjoram, oregano, parsley and garlic and cook, stirring, for 1 minute.

3 Stir in wine and stock, bring to a gentle boil and simmer for 4 minutes. To serve, spoon sauce over hot pasta and toss to combine.

FOREST MUSHROOM PASTA

REALLY EASY!

If you can only get ordinary mushrooms, add a few dried mushrooms for extra flavour. You will need to soak the dried mushrooms in boiling water for 20 minutes or until they are soft. Drain well, then slice or chop and add to the fresh mushrooms when cooking. Dried mushrooms have a strong flavour so you only need a few.

Serves 6
350g (12 oz) pasta of your choice
2 teaspoons vegetable oil
1 clove garlic, crushed
750g (1½ lb) mixed mushrooms, such as Shitake, oyster, chestnut, etc

White Sauce
30g (1 oz) butter
2 tablespoons flour
500 ml (16 fl oz) milk
¼ teaspoon ground nutmeg
freshly ground black pepper

1 Cook pasta in boiling water in a large saucepan, following packet directions. Drain, set aside and keep warm.

2 To make sauce, melt butter in a saucepan over a medium heat. Stir in flour and cook, stirring, for 1 minute. Remove pan from heat and whisk in milk. Return pan to heat and cook, stirring, until sauce boils and thickens. Stir in nutmeg and season to taste with black pepper. Add sauce to pasta and mix to combine. Set aside and keep warm.

3 Heat oil in a frying pan over a medium heat. Add garlic and mushrooms and cook, stirring, for 4 minutes or until mushrooms are soft. To serve, top pasta with mushroom mixture.

PASTA WITH SIX HERB SAUCE • FOREST MUSHROOM PASTA

LOBSTER IN PASTA NESTS

E A S Y !

Pieces of lobster wrapped in cooked, fine pasta and then deep-fried and served with a Lime Cream sauce.

Serves 6

250g (8 oz) angel's hair pasta, or fine spaghetti
3 uncooked lobster tails, shelled and flesh cut into 4 cm
(1½ inch) pieces, or 12 large uncooked tiger prawns,
peeled and deveined
flour
vegetable oil for deep-frying

Lime Cream

125g (4 oz) mayonnaise
60g (2 oz) sour cream
1 tablespoon finely grated lime rind
1 tablespoon lime juice
1 tablespoon whole grain mustard
2 tablespoons chopped fresh tarragon or 1 teaspoon dried
tarragon

1 Cook pasta in boiling water in a large saucepan until almost cooked. Drain, rinse under cold running water, drain again and pat dry on absorbent kitchen paper. Set aside.

2 To make Lime Cream, place mayonnaise, sour cream, lime rind, lime juice, mustard and tarragon in a bowl and mix to combine. Set aside.

3 Dust lobster pieces or prawns, if using, with flour. Wrap a few stands of pasta around each lobster piece. Continue wrapping with pasta to form a net effect around lobster.

4 Heat oil in a large saucepan until a cube of bread,

dropped in, browns in 50 seconds. Cook pasta-wrapped lobster in batches for 2-3 minutes or until golden. Drain on absorbent kitchen paper and serve immediately with Lime Cream.

RAVIOLI WITH WALNUT SAUCE

REALLY EASY!

Take care when making the sauce. Only process it briefly, or until the ingredients are just combined, once the cream is added. If you over process, the cream may separate and cause the sauce to curdle.

Serves 6
750g (1½ lb) cheese and spinach ravioli

Walnut Sauce
200g (7 oz) walnuts
15g (½ oz) fresh basil, leaves removed and stems discarded
45g (1½ oz) butter, softened
45g (1½ oz) grated Parmesan cheese
freshly ground black pepper
100 ml (3½ fl oz) olive oil
150 ml (5 fl oz) double cream

1 Cook ravioli in boiling water in a large saucepan, following packet directions. Drain, set aside and keep warm.

2 To make sauce, place walnuts and basil in a food processor or blender and process until finely chopped. Add butter, Parmesan cheese and black pepper to taste. With machine running, slowly add oil and cream and process until it is just combined. To serve, spoon sauce over pasta and toss.

RASPBERRY AND SALMON PASTA

E A S Y !

**An unusual dish of cooked pasta topped with
salmon and dill and served with a fresh
raspberry mayonnaise.**

Serves 6
500g (1 lb) pepper or plain fettuccine
1 tablespoon vegetable oil
500g (1 lb) salmon fillet, bones and skin removed
2 tablespoons lemon juice
2 tablespoons chopped fresh dill

Raspberry Mayonnaise
200g (7 oz) raspberries
250g (8 oz) mayonnaise
2 teaspoons whole grain mustard
1 tablespoon lemon juice

1 To make mayonnaise, place raspberries in a food processor or blender and process until smooth. Push purée through a fine plastic sieve and discard seeds. Add mayonnaise, mustard and lemon juice to purée, mix to combine and set aside.

2 Cook pasta in boiling water in a large saucepan, following packet directions. Drain, set aside and keep warm.

3 Heat oil in a frying pan over a medium heat. Brush salmon with lemon juice and sprinkle with dill. Place salmon in pan and cook for 2-3 minutes each side or until flesh flakes when tested with a fork. Remove salmon from pan and cut into thick slices.

4 To serve, divide pasta between six serving plates. Top with salmon slices and drizzle with raspberry mayonnaise. Serve immediately.

TOMATO PASTA ROLLS

**Freshly made pasta rolled out and then spread
with spinach, eggs and cheese and thinly sliced
ham. It is rolled up like a Swiss roll and cooked,
then allowed to cool before slicing and serving.
These rolls make an ideal finger food or serve
with a small green salad as a colourful first
course for a dinner party.**

Serves 6
125g (4 oz) flour
1 egg
1 tablespoon water
1 tablespoon concentrated tomato purée
1-2 teaspoons olive oil

Spinach Filling
250g (8 oz) frozen spinach, thawed and well drained
180g (6 oz) ricotta or cottage cheese
1 egg
45g (1½ oz) grated Parmesan cheese
½ teaspoon ground nutmeg
freshly ground black pepper
6 slices prosciutto or thinly sliced ham
250g (8 oz) sliced mozzarella cheese

1 Place flour, egg, water, tomato purée and oil in a food
processor and process to combine. Turn dough onto a
lightly floured surface and knead for 5 minutes or until
dough is smooth and elastic. Wrap dough in plastic food
wrap and set aside to stand for 15 minutes.

2 To make filling, place spinach, ricotta cheese, egg,
Parmesan cheese, nutmeg and black pepper to taste in a
bowl, and mix to combine.

3 Roll out the dough to form a rectangle 30 x 45 cm

(12 x 18 inch.) Spread with the filling mixture, leaving a 2.5 cm (1 inch) border, then top with the prosciutto or ham and the mozzarella cheese. Fold in borders on long sides, then roll up from the short side. Wrap roll in a piece of washed calico cloth or oiled foil and secure ends with string.

4 Half fill a baking dish with water and place on the stove top. Bring to the boil, add roll, reduce heat, cover dish with aluminium foil or lid and simmer for 30 minutes. Turn roll once or twice during cooking. Remove roll from water and allow to cool for 5 minutes. Remove calico from roll and refrigerate until firm. To serve, cut roll into slices.

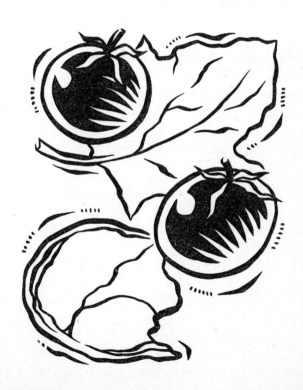

TOMATO PASTA ROLLS

CAVIAR FETTUCCINE

REALLY EASY!

**Cooked fettuccine tossed with red and black
caviar and chopped hard-boiled eggs, and served
topped with sour cream.**

Serves 4

300g (10 oz) fettuccine
2 tablespoons olive oil
2 cloves garlic, crushed
2 tablespoons finely snipped fresh chives
3 tablespoons red caviar, or lump fish roe
3 tablespoons black caviar, or lump fish roe
2 hard-boiled eggs, chopped
4 tablespoons sour cream

1 Cook fettuccine in boiling water in a large saucepan, following packet directions. Drain, set aside and keep warm.

2 Heat oil in a large frying pan and cook garlic over a low heat for 2-3 minutes. Add fettuccine, chives, red and black caviar, and eggs to pan. Toss to combine. Serve immediately, topped with sour cream.

PASTA
WITH VEGETABLES

Cooked pasta tossed with freshly cooked vegetables or topped with a rich vegetable sauce makes a wonderful meal that needs little else to complete it. Even those who are not vegetarians will be inspired to cook a few of these recipes from time to time as we all should serve meatless meals once in a while.

GRILLED VEGETABLE PASTA

EASY!

 Fresh pasta topped with grilled mixed peppers, aubergines and tomatoes.

Serves 4

1 red pepper, de-seeded and cut into quarters
1 yellow pepper, de-seeded and cut into quarters
1 green pepper, de-seeded and cut into quarters
6 baby aubergines, cut lengthwise into quarters
2 tablespoons olive oil
8 plum tomatoes, halved
1 red onion, sliced
2 cloves garlic, crushed
1 tablespoon chopped fresh purple basil or green basil
freshly ground black pepper
500g (1 lb) fresh spinach tagliatelle

1 Place red, yellow and green pepper quarters, skin side up, under a preheated hot grill and cook for 5-10 minutes until skins are blistered and charred. Place peppers in a plastic food bag and set aside until cool enough to handle. Remove skins from peppers and cut flesh into thick slices.

2 Brush cut surfaces of aubergines lightly with oil and cook under preheated hot grill for 2-3 minutes each side or until golden. Place tomatoes, skin side down, under preheated hot grill and cook for 2 minutes or until soft.

3 Heat remaining oil in a frying pan over a medium heat, add onion and garlic and cook, stirring, for 4 minutes or until onion is soft and golden. Add red pepper, yellow pepper, green pepper, aubergines, tomatoes, basil and black pepper to taste and cook, stirring, for 4 minutes.

4 Cook pasta in boiling water in a large saucepan, following packet directions. Drain well, top with vegetable mixture and serve immediately.

TORTELLINI BOSCAIOLA

E A S Y !

**Cheese and spinach tortellini topped with a
creamy sauce of onions and mushrooms.**

Serves 6
*750g (1½ lb) cheese and spinach filled tortellini
grated Parmesan cheese (optional)*

Creamy Mushroom Sauce
*15g (½ oz) butter
4 spring onions, chopped
250g (8 oz) mushrooms, sliced
250 ml (8 fl oz) vegetable or chicken stock
500 ml (16 fl oz) double cream
freshly ground black pepper*

1 Cook pasta in boiling water in a large saucepan, following packet directions. Drain, set aside and keep warm.

2 To make sauce, melt butter in a frying pan over a medium heat. Add spring onions and mushrooms and cook, stirring, for 4 minutes or until mushrooms are soft.

3 Stir in stock, cream and black pepper to taste, bring to a gentle boil and simmer for 6-8 minutes or until sauce reduces and thickens slightly.

4 To serve, spoon sauce over hot pasta, toss to combine and top with Parmesan cheese, if using.

GRILLED VEGETABLE PASTA • TORTELLINI BOSCAIOLA

VEGETABLE CANNELLONI

Cannelloni tubes filled with leek, spinach, ricotta and sweetcorn, topped with a tomato sauce and baked in the oven.

Serves 4
12 instant (oven-ready) cannelloni tubes
250g (8 oz) mozzarella cheese, grated

Leek and Spinach Filling
2 teaspoons olive oil
1 clove garlic, crushed
2 spring onions, finely chopped
2 leeks, thinly sliced
1 red pepper, sliced
500g (1 lb) young spinach, chopped
200g (7 oz) ricotta cheese, drained
300g (10 oz) canned creamed sweet corn
2 teaspoons paprika

Tomato Sauce
1 teaspoon olive oil
1 onion, chopped
400g (14 oz) tomato passata
2 tablespoons dry white wine

1 To make filling, heat oil in a frying pan over a medium heat. Add garlic, spring onions and leeks and cook, stirring, for 4 minutes or until leeks are soft.

2 Add red pepper and spinach and cook, stirring, for 3 minutes or until spinach wilts. Drain off liquid.

3 Transfer vegetable mixture to a large bowl, add ricotta cheese, sweet corn and paprika and mix well to combine.

4 Spoon filling into cannelloni tubes and place tubes

side by side in a large greased ovenproof dish. Set aside. Preheat oven to 180C,350F,Gas 4.

5 To make sauce, heat oil in a saucepan over a medium heat. Add onion and cook, stirring, for 3 minutes or until onion is soft. Stir in tomato passata and wine, bring to a gentle boil and simmer for 4 minutes. Pour sauce over cannelloni tubes, sprinkle with mozzarella cheese and bake for 40 minutes or until pasta is tender and cheese is golden.

VEGETABLE CANNELLONI

CANNELLONI WITH PESTO CREAM

Cannelloni made with spinach lasagne sheets, filled with spinach, mushrooms and tomato passata, topped with a Pesto Cream and baked in the oven.

Serves 4
16 sheets fresh spinach lasagne

Spinach Filling
2 teaspoons olive oil
1 onion, chopped
2 cloves garlic, crushed
12 leaves spinach, shredded
250g (8 oz) button mushrooms, finely chopped
250 ml (8 fl oz) tomato passata

Pesto Cream
180g (6 oz) ready-made pesto
300g (10 oz) sour cream
200g (7 oz) natural yogurt
freshly ground black pepper

1 To make filling, heat oil in a frying pan over a medium heat, add onion and garlic and cook, stirring, for 3 minutes or until onion is soft. Add spinach and mushrooms and cook for 4 minutes longer. Stir in tomato passata, bring to a gentle boil and simmer, stirring occasionally, for 10-15 minutes or until liquid evaporates.

2 To make Pesto Cream, place pesto, sour cream, yogurt and black pepper to taste in a bowl and mix to combine. Preheat oven to 180C, 350F, Gas 4.

3 Cook lasagne sheets in boiling water in a .large

saucepan following packet directions. Drain well.

4 Place spoonfuls of filling along one long edge of each lasagne sheet and roll up. Place rolls join side down in a greased oven proof dish and spoon over Pesto Cream. Bake for 25-30 minutes or until hot and bubbling.

CANNELLONI WITH PESTO CREAM

CHILLI PASTA BAKE

R E A L L Y   E A S Y !

Penne pasta cooked and mixed with sour cream, put in a baking dish, topped with a chilli, bean and tomato sauce, sprinkled with cheese and baked.

Serves 4
350g (12 oz) penne pasta
300g (10 oz) sour cream
125g (4 oz) mature Cheddar cheese , grated

Chilli Sauce
2 teaspoons vegetable oil
2 onions, chopped
1 teaspoon ground cumin
1 teaspoon ground coriander
½ teaspoon chilli powder
400g (14 oz) canned red kidney beans, drained
400g (14 oz) tomato passata

1 Cook pasta in boiling water in a large saucepan, following packet directions. Drain, stir in sour cream and spread over base of an ovenproof dish. Preheat oven to 180C, 350F,Gas 4.

2 To make sauce, heat oil in a large saucepan. Add onions and cook over a medium heat, stirring, for 3 minutes or until onions are soft. Add cumin, coriander and chilli powder and cook, stirring constantly, for 1 minute longer. Stir in beans and tomato passata, bring to the boil and simmer for 5 minutes.

3 Pour sauce over pasta, sprinkle with cheese and bake for 15-20 minutes or until cheese melts and is golden.

SPAGHETTI WITH RATATOUILLE SAUCE

REALLY EASY!

**A vegetarian spaghetti bolognese, with a
ratatouille sauce replacing the meat.**

Serves 4
500g (1 lb) wholemeal spaghetti
4 tablespoons grated Parmesan cheese

Ratatouille Sauce
1 aubergine, diced
1 large onion, sliced
1 clove garlic, crushed
1 green pepper, diced
2 courgettes, diced
*500g (1 lb) tomatoes, skinned, de-seeded and roughly
chopped*
125 ml (4 fl oz) dry white wine
1 tablespoon finely chopped fresh basil
½ teaspoon dried thyme
½ teaspoon dried oregano
freshly ground black pepper

1 To make sauce, place aubergine, onion, garlic, green pepper, courgettes, tomatoes, wine, basil, thyme and oregano in a non-stick frying pan, and cook over a low heat, stirring occasionally, for 30-45 minutes or until mixture forms a thick sauce. Season to taste with black pepper.

2 Cook spaghetti in boiling water in a large saucepan, following packet directions. Drain spaghetti, spoon sauce over, toss to combine and sprinkle with Parmesan cheese.

WHOLEMEAL SPAGHETTI WITH TOMATOES AND ASPARAGUS

REALLY EASY!

The 'nutty' taste of wholemeal spaghetti goes well with the thick, chunky sauce of garlic, tomatoes, asparagus and parsley.

Serves 4
500g wholemeal spaghetti

Sauce
1 tablespoon olive oil
1 clove garlic, crushed
400g (14 oz) canned tomatoes, drained and chopped
300g (10 oz) canned asparagus tips, drained
1 tablespoon chopped fresh parsley
1 tablespoon brown sugar
2 tablespoons red wine

1 Cook spaghetti in boiling water, following the packet instructions. Drain and keep warm.

2 To make sauce, heat oil in a frying pan, cook garlic for 1 minute. Stir in tomatoes, asparagus, parsley, sugar and wine and season to taste. Cover and simmer for 15-20 minutes. Spoon sauce over hot spaghetti and serve with Parmesan cheese if desired.

HERB AND VEGETABLE FETTUCCINE

EASY!

This delicious combination of vegetables and prosciutto takes next to no time to prepare and is one of those wonderful one-dish meals. You might like to serve it with crusty French bread or wholemeal rolls.

Serves 4

30g (1 oz) dried mushrooms
boiling water
250g (8 oz) fettuccine
2 tablespoons olive oil
2 cloves garlic, crushed
250g (8 oz) asparagus, cut into 2.5 cm (1 inch) lengths
1 red pepper, de-seeded and chopped
30g (1 oz) small basil leaves
1 tablespoon lemon juice
freshly ground black pepper
4 tablespoons grated Parmesan cheese

1 Place mushrooms in a bowl and cover with boiling water. Set aside to soak for 20 minutes or until mushrooms are tender. Drain, remove stalks if necessary and chop mushrooms.

2 Cook fettuccine in boiling water in a large saucepan, following packet directions. Drain, set aside and keep warm.

3 Heat oil in a large frying pan and cook mushrooms and garlic over a medium heat for 2 minutes. Add asparagus and red pepper and cook for 2-3 minutes longer.

4 Stir in basil leaves, lemon juice and fettuccine and cook, tossing, for 3-4 minutes or until heated. Season to taste with black pepper and serve immediately, topped with Parmesan cheese.

PENNE NAPOLITANA

REALLY EASY!

**Cooked pasta with a tomato, wine
and herb sauce.**

Serves 4

500g (1 lb) penne
fresh Parmesan cheese

Napolitana Sauce

2 teaspoons olive oil
2 onions, chopped
2 cloves garlic, crushed
*2 x 400g (14 oz) canned tomatoes, undrained and
mashed*
180 ml (6 fl oz) red wine
1 tablespoon chopped flat-leaf parsley
*1 tablespoon chopped fresh oregano or ½ teaspoon dried
oregano*
freshly ground black pepper

1 Cook pasta in boiling water in a large saucepan, following packet directions. Drain, set aside and keep warm.

2 To make sauce, heat oil in a saucepan over a medium heat. Add onions and garlic and cook, stirring, for 3 minutes or until onions are soft.

3 Stir in tomatoes, wine, parsley, oregano and black pepper to taste, bring to a gentle boil and simmer for 15 minutes or until sauce reduces and thickens.

4 To serve, spoon sauce over hot pasta and top with shavings of Parmesan cheese.

FARFALLE WITH SPRING VEGETABLES

REALLY EASY!

Cooked bow shaped pasta mixed with broccoli, asparagus and mangetout, with a creamy sauce and fresh mint.

Serves 4

500g (1 Ib) farfalle (bow shaped pasta)
15g (½ oz) butter
2 spring onions, finely chopped
1 teaspoon finely grated orange rind
375 ml (12 fl oz) double cream
250 ml (8 fl oz) vegetable stock
250g (8 oz) broccoli, cut into florets
250g (8 oz) asparagus spears, cut into 4 cm (1½ inch)
lengths
125g (4 oz) mangetout
1 tablespoon finely chopped fresh mint
30g (1 oz) pine kernels, toasted

1 Cook pasta in boiling water in a large saucepan, following packet directions. Drain, set aside and keep warm.

2 Melt butter in a frying pan over a medium heat. Add spring onions and cook, stirring, for 2 minutes. Stir in orange rind, cream and stock, bring to a gentle boil and simmer for 10 minutes.

3 Add broccoli, asparagus, mangetout and mint to cream mixture and cook, stirring occasionally, for 5 minutes or until vegetables are tender. To serve, spoon vegetable mixture over hot pasta, toss to combine and sprinkle with pine kernels.

PENNE NAPOLITANA • FARFALLE WITH SPRING VEGETABLES

MEXICAN CHILLI PASTA

REALLY EASY!

Fresh, flavoured fettuccine with a sauce of chillies, tomatoes and red kidney beans.

Serves 4
750g (1½ lb) fresh tomato or spinach fettuccine

Mexican Chilli Sauce
2 onions, chopped
1 clove garlic, crushed
2 red chillies, finely chopped
1 tablespoon water
400 ml (14 fl oz) tomato passata
400g (14 oz) canned red kidney beans, drained

1 Cook fettuccine in boiling water in a large saucepan, following packet directions. Drain and set aside to keep warm.

2 To make sauce, cook onions, garlic, chillies and water in large saucepan for 3-4 minutes, or until onion is soft. Stir in tomato passata and red kidney beans, bring to the boil, then reduce heat and simmer for 4-5 minutes, or until sauce thickens. Spoon sauce over pasta and serve.

NUTTY VERMICELLI WITH BROCCOLI

REALLY EASY!

The crunch of almonds, the fresh taste of broccoli and a touch of chilli make a superb combination when teamed with vermicelli in this quick and easy, light meal.

Serves 4

500g (1 lb) vermicelli noodles
250g (8 oz) broccoli, broken into florets
30g (1 oz) butter
4 spring onions, finely chopped
2 cloves garlic, crushed
1 teaspoon chilli paste (sambal oelek)
60g (2 oz) blanched almonds, chopped
60 ml (2 fl oz) white wine
freshly ground black pepper

1 Cook vermicelli in boiling water in a large saucepan, following packet directions. Drain, set aside and keep warm.

2 Boil, steam or microwave broccoli until just tender. Drain and refresh under cold running water. Drain again and set aside. Melt butter in a large frying pan and cook spring onions, garlic, chilli paste (sambal oelek) and almonds, stirring, over a medium heat for 2 minutes. Stir in wine and cook for 3 minutes longer. Add broccoli and vermicelli, toss to combine and cook for 3-4 minutes. Season to taste with black pepper.

MEXICAN CHILLI PASTA • NUTTY VERMICELLI WITH BROCCOLI

BAKED VEGETABLE PAPPARDELLE

If you can't find wide ribbon pasta, simply cut fresh or cooked lasagne into wide strips.

Serves 6
3 large aubergines, thinly sliced
salt
3 tablespoons olive oil
1 onion, chopped
2 cloves garlic, crushed
2 x 400g (14 oz) canned tomatoes, undrained and mashed
½ teaspoon sugar
freshly ground black pepper
350g (12 oz) pappardelle (very wide ribbon pasta)
300g (10 oz) mascarpone or ricotta cheese
200g (7 oz) grated mozzarella cheese

1 Sprinkle aubergine slices with salt, place in a colander and drain for 10 minutes. Rinse under cold running water and pat dry.

2 Place all but 2 teaspoons of oil in a frying pan and put over a medium heat. Cook aubergine slices a few at a time for 3-4 minutes each side or until golden. Add more oil if necessary. Drain on absorbent kitchen paper.

3 Heat remaining oil in a frying pan, add onion and garlic and cook, stirring, for 3 minutes or until onion is soft. Stir in tomatoes, sugar and black pepper to taste. Bring to a gentle boil and simmer, stirring occasionally, for 15 minutes or until mixture reduces and thickens.

4 Preheat oven to 220C,425F,Gas 7. Cook pasta in boiling water in a large saucepan for 10 minutes or until almost cooked. Drain well. Add tomato mixture to pasta and toss to combine.

5 Spread half the pasta mixture over the base of a lightly greased 2 litre (3½ pint) ovenproof dish. Top with half the aubergine slices, half the mascarpone or ricotta cheese and half the mozzarella cheese. Repeat layers, finishing with a layer of mozzarella cheese and bake in the oven for 20 minutes or until hot and bubbling.

MACARONI WITH BASIL

REALLY EASY!

Macaroni tossed with mushrooms, sun-dried tomatoes and basil.

Serves 4
350g (12 oz) wholemeal macaroni
1 tablespoon olive oil
2 cloves garlic, crushed
250g (8 oz) button mushrooms, sliced
6 sun-dried tomatoes, drained and cut into strips
2 tablespoons chopped fresh basil
freshly ground black pepper

1 Cook macaroni in boiling water in a large saucepan, following packet directions. Drain, set aside and keep warm.

2 Heat oil in a large frying pan and cook garlic, mushrooms and tomatoes over a medium heat for 4-5 minutes. Stir in basil and season to taste with black pepper.

3 Add macaroni to mushroom mixture and toss to combine. Serve immediately.

TAGLIATELLE WITH SPINACH AND MUSHROOMS

REALLY EASY!

Freshly cooked tomato tagliatelle and spinach, with a mushroom, cream and Marsala sauce.

Serves 4

500g (1 lb) fresh tomato tagliatelle
60g (2 oz) butter
1 clove garlic, crushed
2 tablespoons Marsala
250g (8 oz) button mushrooms, sliced
250 ml (8 fl oz) double cream
freshly ground black pepper
750g (1½ lb) fresh spinach leaves, shredded
grated fresh Parmesan cheese

1 Cook tagliatelle in boiling water in a large saucepan until 'al dente'. Drain, set aside and keep warm.

2 Melt butter in a saucepan and cook garlic and Marsala over a low heat for 3 minutes or until syrupy. Add mushrooms and cook for 3 minutes longer. Blend in cream and bring to the boil. Season to taste with black pepper.

3 Add pasta to sauce. Toss in spinach and stir to coat. Cook over a low heat for 2-3 minutes or until spinach is warmed through. Serve with Parmesan cheese.

MACARONI WITH BASIL • TAGLIATELLE WITH SPINACH & MUSHROOMS

PASTA WITH AVOCADO AND LIME SAUCE

REALLY EASY!

Cooked pasta with mangetout and courgettes, mixed with a sauce of avocado, ricotta, lime and coriander.

Serves 6

500g (1 lb) pasta shapes of your choice
125g (4 oz) mangetout, trimmed
125g (4 oz) courgettes, sliced
shavings of fresh Parmesan cheese (optional)

Avocado Sauce

1 avocado, stoned and peeled
250g (8 oz) ricotta cheese, drained
1 tablespoon lime juice
2 teaspoons finely grated lime rind
2 tablespoons milk
2 tablespoons fresh chopped coriander
freshly ground black pepper

1 Cook pasta in boiling water in a large saucepan, following packet instructions. Drain, set aside and keep warm.

2 To make sauce, place avocado, ricotta cheese, lime juice, lime rind, milk, coriander and black pepper to taste in a food processor or blender and process until smooth. Set aside.

3 Boil, steam or microwave the mangetout and courgettes separately until just tender. Drain well. Add vegetables to hot pasta and toss to combine. To serve, top pasta with sauce and shavings of Parmesan cheese, if using.

BEAN LASAGNE

EASY!

 A non-meat lasagne with a Tomato Bean Sauce, spinach, and a cheese topping.

Serves 6
12 spinach leaves, chopped
250g (8 oz) lasagne sheets
125g (4 oz) Cheddar cheese, grated
2 tablespoons grated Parmesan cheese

Tomato Bean Sauce
1 tablespoon olive oil
2 onions, chopped
2 cloves garlic, crushed
400g (14 oz) canned tomatoes, undrained
400g (14 oz) canned butter beans, drained and puréed
400g (14 oz) canned red kidney beans, drained
1 teaspoon hot chilli sauce
1 teaspoon dried oregano

1 To make sauce, heat oil in a large frying pan and cook onions and garlic for 4-5 minutes or until onions are soft. Stir in remaining sauce ingredients. Bring to the boil, then reduce heat and simmer, uncovered, for 10 minutes or until sauce reduces and thickens. Remove from heat and set aside.

2 Place a little water in a saucepan and bring to the boil, add spinach and cook for 1-2 minutes or until spinach wilts. Drain and set aside. Cook lasagne sheets as directed on packet. Drain. Preheat oven to 180C,350F,Gas 4.

3 Place one-third of the lasagne sheets in the base of a lightly greased, shallow ovenproof dish, then top with one-third of the bean sauce and half of the spinach. Repeat layers, then finish with a layer of lasagne sheets and remaining bean sauce. Sprinkle with cheeses. Bake for 30 minutes or until heated through and golden.

VEGETABLE CHILLI PASTA

EASY!

Pasta shells and aubergines with a sauce of onions, chillies, garlic, tomatoes, and basil.

Serves 4
2 aubergines
salt
500g (1 lb) pasta shells
60 ml (2 fl oz) olive oil
2 onions, chopped
2 fresh red chillies, de-seeded and chopped
2 cloves garlic, crushed
2 x 400g (14 oz) canned tomatoes, undrained and mashed
125ml (4 fl oz) dry white wine
2 tablespoons chopped fresh basil or 1 teaspoon dried basil

1 Cut aubergines into 2 cm (¾ inch) cubes. Place in a colander, sprinkle with salt and set aside to drain for 10 minutes. Rinse aubergines under cold running water and pat dry.

2 Cook pasta in boiling water in a large saucepan, following packet directions. Drain, set aside and keep warm.

3 Heat oil in a large frying pan over a medium heat and cook aubergines in batches for 5 minutes or until golden. Remove aubergines from pan, drain on kitchen paper and set aside.

4 Add onions, chillies and garlic to pan and cook, stirring, for 3 minutes or until onions are golden. Stir in tomatoes, wine and basil, bring to a gentle boil and simmer for 5 minutes. To serve, put pasta and aubergines into a dish and spoon over the hot sauce.

PASTA
WITH CHEESE

When you think of pasta and cheese,
Macaroni Cheese immediately springs to mind.
Pasta marries well with many other cheeses
such as blue cheese, ricotta and feta. In fact
most cheese that you can cook with, will
go well with pasta.

BLUE CHEESE PENNE

REALLY EASY!

Cooked pasta with a tangy blue cheese sauce.

Serves 6
500g (1 lb) penne

Blue Cheese Sauce
250 ml (8 fl oz) double cream
180g (6 oz) blue cheese, crumbled
3 tablespoons grated fresh Parmesan cheese
freshly ground black pepper

1 Cook penne in boiling water in a large saucepan, following packet directions. Drain, set aside and keep warm.

2 To make sauce, place cream and blue cheese in a saucepan, bring to the boil, stirring constantly, over a medium heat. As soon as the mixture reaches the boil, remove from heat and pour over pasta. Sprinkle with Parmesan cheese, season to taste with black pepper and toss to combine. Serve immediately.

TUNA AND RED PEPPER FILLED SHELLS

REALLY EASY!

These giant shells filled with tuna and cheese are fun to eat hot, or cold as finger food, or they can be served with a sauce as a first course.

Makes 16 filled shells
16 giant pasta shells

Filling
250g (8 oz) ricotta cheese, drained
400g (14 oz) canned tuna in brine, drained and flaked
½ red pepper, diced
1 tablespoon chopped capers
1 teaspoon snipped fresh chives
4 tablespoons grated Cheddar or Gruyère cheese
pinch ground (or freshly grated) nutmeg
freshly ground black pepper
2 tablespoons grated fresh Parmesan cheese

1 Cook 8 pasta shells in a large saucepan of boiling water until 'al dente'. Drain, rinse under cold water and drain again. Set aside, not overlapping. Repeat with remaining shells.

2 To make filling, place ricotta cheese and tuna in a bowl and mix to combine. Mix in red pepper, capers, chives, 2 tablespoons grated cheese, nutmeg, and pepper to taste.

3 Fill each shell with ricotta mixture and place in a shallow ovenproof dish. Sprinkle with remaining grated cheese and Parmesan cheese. Place under a preheated grill and cook until cheese melts.

RICOTTA AND BASIL LASAGNE

EASY!

**For a complete meal, serve this lasagne
with whole grain bread or rolls and a
tossed green salad.**

Serves 6
4 aubergines, sliced
salt
olive oil
1 bunch fresh basil, leaves removed from stems
500g (1 lb) ricotta cheese, drained
300g (10 oz) mozzarella cheese, sliced

Tomato Sauce
2 teaspoons vegetable oil
2 onions, chopped
2 cloves garlic, crushed
*2 x 400g (14 oz) canned tomatoes, undrained and
mashed*
125 ml (4 fl oz) red wine
2 teaspoons sugar

1 Place aubergine slices in a colander set over a bowl
and sprinkle with salt. Set aside to stand for 10 minutes,
then rinse under cold running water and pat dry with
absorbent kitchen paper.

2 Brush aubergine slices with oil and cook under a
preheated medium grill for 2-4 minutes each side or until
golden.

3 To make sauce, heat oil in a saucepan, add onions and
garlic and cook over a medium heat, stirring constantly,
for 3 minutes or until onions are soft. Stir in tomatoes,
wine and sugar, bring to the boil and simmer for 10
minutes or until sauce reduces and thickens.

4 Preheat the oven to 190C, 375F, Gas 5. Line the base of an ovenproof dish with one-third of the aubergine slices, top with one-third of the basil leaves, one-third of the tomato sauce, one-third of the ricotta cheese and one-third of the mozzarella cheese. Repeat layers, finishing with a layer of mozzarella cheese. Bake for 30 minutes or until hot and bubbling and top is golden.

RICOTTA AND BASIL LASAGNE

TOMATO AND CHEESE LASAGNE

EASY!

If instant (oven-ready) lasagne is unavailable use dried lasagne instead, but cook it briefly before using. When using instant (oven-ready) lasagne, the cooked dish tends to be more moist and the pasta more tender if the lasagne sheets are dipped in warm water before assembling lasagne.

Serves 6

250g (8 oz) ricotta cheese, drained
1 tablespoon chopped fresh parsley
1 tablespoon chopped fresh basil
freshly ground black pepper
60g (2 oz) grated pecorino or Parmesan cheese
125g (4 oz) grated mozzarella cheese
9 sheets instant (oven-ready) lasagne

Fresh Tomato Sauce

2 teaspoons olive oil
2 cloves garlic, crushed
1 onion, chopped
8 ripe tomatoes, skinned, de-seeded and chopped
2 tablespoons tomato purée
1 bay leaf
3 sprigs fresh thyme or ½ teaspoon dried thyme
1 small ham or bacon bone
125 ml (4 fl oz) water
1 teaspoon sugar

1 Place ricotta cheese, parsley, basil and black pepper to taste in a bowl and mix to combine. Set aside.

2 Place pecorino or Parmesan and mozzarella cheeses in a bowl and mix to combine. Set aside.

3 To make sauce, heat oil in a saucepan over a medium

heat, add garlic and onion and cook, stirring, for 3 minutes or until onion is soft. Add tomatoes and cook, stirring, for 4 minutes longer.

4 Add tomato purée, bay leaf, thyme, ham or bacon bone, water and sugar and bring to the boil. Reduce heat and simmer, stirring occasionally, for 45 minutes or until sauce reduces and thickens. Remove ham or bacon bone and bay leaf from sauce and discard.

5 Preheat oven to 180C,350F,Gas 4. Place three lasagne sheets in the base of a greased 18 x 28 cm (7 x 11 inch) ovenproof dish. Top with one-third of the tomato sauce, then one-third of the ricotta mixture and one-third of the cheese mixture. Repeat layers twice more to use all ingredients finishing with a layer of cheese. Bake for 30 minutes or until hot and bubbling and top is golden.

TOMATO AND CHEESE LASAGNE

PASTA WITH GORGONZOLA AND WALNUT SAUCE

[V]

REALLY EASY!

Fresh cooked pasta with a Gorgonzola, cream and walnut sauce.

Serves 6
500g (1 lb) fresh pasta

Gorgonzola Sauce
200g (7 oz) Gorgonzola or blue cheese, crumbled
180 ml (6 fl oz) milk
60g (2 oz) butter
90g (3 oz) chopped walnuts
200 ml (7 fl oz) double cream
freshly ground black pepper

1 Cook pasta in boiling water in a large saucepan, following packet directions. Drain, set aside and keep warm.

2 To make sauce, place Gorgonzola or blue cheese, milk and butter in a saucepan and cook over a low heat, stirring, for 4-5 minutes or until cheese melts. Stir in walnuts, cream and black pepper to taste, bring to a gentle boil and simmer for 5 minutes or until sauce reduces and thickens. Spoon sauce over hot pasta and toss to combine.

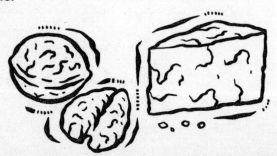

PASTA WITH CHICKPEAS AND FETA

REALLY EASY!

**Serve this dish warm, or cold as a pasta salad.
Cold cooked chickpeas can be used instead of
canned chickpeas**

Serves 6
500g (1 lb) dried ribbon pasta

Chickpea and Feta Sauce
*2 x 400g (14 oz) canned chickpeas, drained
6 tomatoes, chopped
300g (10 oz) feta cheese, roughly chopped
90 ml (3 fl oz) balsamic vinegar
3 tablespoons chopped fresh mixed herbs
8 sun-dried tomatoes, chopped
1 tablespoon capers, drained (optional)*

1 Cook pasta in boiling water in a large saucepan, following packet directions. Drain, set aside and keep warm.

2 Place chickpeas, tomatoes, cheese, vinegar, herbs, sun-dried tomatoes and capers in a bowl and mix to combine. Toss chickpea mixture with warm pasta.

PASTA WITH GORGONZOLA & WALNUT SAUCE • PASTA WITH CHICKPEAS & FETA

MACARONI CHEESE

EASY!

You can vary this popular family favourite by adding chopped ham, chopped red or green peppers, finely chopped onion or chopped fresh parsley to the sauce.

Serves 4

300g (10 oz) macaroni
125g (4 oz) tasty cheese (mature Cheddar), grated

Cheese Sauce

75g (2½ oz) butter
45g (1½ oz) flour
1 teaspoon dry mustard powder
600 ml (1 pint) milk
90g (3 oz) tasty cheese (mature Cheddar), grated
freshly black ground pepper

1 Cook pasta in boiling water in a large saucepan, following packet directions. Drain well and turn into a large greased, ovenproof dish.

2 Preheat oven to 180C,350F,Gas 4. To make sauce, melt butter in a saucepan over a medium heat. Stir in flour and mustard and cook, stirring, for 1 minute. Remove pan from heat and whisk in milk. Return pan to heat and cook, stirring, for 3-4 minutes or until sauce boils and thickens. Stir in cheese and black pepper to taste.

3 Pour sauce over pasta, sprinkle with cheese and bake for 20-25 minutes or until hot and bubbling and top is golden.

PASTA
WITH CHICKEN

Chicken and pasta are both fairly bland
and so they work well together in a subtle
way, as in Chicken Cannelloni. Equally, they
make a good base for strong or spicy flavours,
as in Cajun Chicken Fettuccine. Chicken livers
are an especially good addition to pasta as they
are tasty and quick to cook and are a useful
standby if bought frozen.

CHICKEN AND LEEK ROLLS

REALLY EASY!

Spinach lasagne filled with chicken and leeks.

Serves 4
12 spinach lasagne sheets
2 tablespoons grated fresh Parmesan cheese

Chicken And Leek Filling
2 teaspoons vegetable oil
3 leeks, finely sliced
3 chicken breast fillets, cut into thin strips
125 ml (4 fl oz) chicken stock
1 tablespoon cornflour blended with 2 tablespoons water
1 teaspoon French mustard
2 teaspoons chopped fresh basil
freshly ground black pepper

1 Cook lasagne sheets in boiling water in a large saucepan until tender. Drain, set aside and keep warm.

2 To make filling, heat oil in a large frying pan and cook leeks and chicken, stirring, for 4-5 minutes or until chicken is brown. Stir in stock, cornflour mixture, mustard and basil and cook, stirring, for 2 minutes longer. Season to taste with black pepper.

3 Place spoonfuls of filling on lasagne sheets, roll up, top with Parmesan cheese and serve immediately.

CAJUN CHICKEN FETTUCCINE

EASY!

A spicy mixture of fettuccine and chicken with a tomato, chilli and green pepper salsa.

Serves 8
2 tablespoons paprika
2 cloves garlic, crushed
2 teaspoons crushed black peppercorns
1 tablespoon ground cumin
1 tablespoon ground coriander
½ teaspoon chilli powder
6 boneless chicken breast fillets, sliced
2 teaspoons vegetable oil
750g (1½ lb) fettuccine

Tomato Salsa
6 ripe tomatoes, chopped
2 fresh red chillies, de-seeded and finely chopped
1 green pepper, chopped
1 tablespoon brown sugar
3 tablespoons balsamic or red wine vinegar

1 To make salsa, place tomatoes, chillies, green pepper, sugar and vinegar in a bowl and toss to combine. Set aside.

2 Place paprika, garlic, black peppercorns, cumin, coriander and chilli powder in a bowl and mix to combine. Add chicken and toss to coat with spice mixture. Heat oil in a frying pan over a medium heat, add chicken and cook, stirring, for 5 minutes or until chicken is tender. Remove chicken from pan, set aside and keep warm.

3 Cook pasta in boiling water in a large saucepan, following packet directions. Drain well and place in a serving dish. Add chicken, toss to combine and serve with salsa.

CHICKEN AND LEEK ROLLS • CAJUN CHICKEN FETTUCCINE

75

CHICKEN LIVERS AND MUSHROOMS ON SPAGHETTI

EASY!

Spaghetti layered with a tomato and onion sauce and a Chicken Liver Sauce and topped with Parmesan cheese. This is a variation of a sauce created for the great singer Caruso.

Serves 4
500g (1 lb) spaghetti
1 tablespoon vegetable oil
90g (3 oz) grated fresh Parmesan cheese

Tomato Sauce
1 tablespoon vegetable oil
30g (1 oz) butter
1 onion, finely diced
2 cloves garlic, crushed
12 small button mushrooms, halved
400g (14 oz) canned tomatoes, undrained and mashed
1 teaspoon sugar
300 ml (½ pint) chicken stock
freshly ground black pepper

Chicken Liver Sauce
30g (1 oz) butter
250g (8 oz) chicken livers, trimmed and sliced
1 teaspoon finely chopped fresh thyme, or ¼ teaspoon dried thyme
90 ml (3 fl oz) Marsala
1 tablespoon finely chopped fresh parsley

1 To make Tomato Sauce, heat oil and butter in a frying pan, and cook onion until soft. Add garlic and mushrooms and cook for 2-3 minutes longer. Then combine tomatoes and sugar and add to mushrooms. Cook over a low heat for 10 minutes. Stir in stock and simmer for 30 minutes longer or until sauce reduces and thickens. Season to taste with black pepper.

2 To make Chicken Liver Sauce, melt butter in a saucepan and cook chicken livers and thyme over a medium heat until brown. Increase heat, stir in Marsala and cook for 1-2 minutes. Stir in parsley.

3 Cook spaghetti in boiling water in a large saucepan until 'al dente'. Drain and toss with the oil.

4 Arrange half spaghetti on a warm serving platter, top with half chicken liver mixture, then half Tomato Sauce. Sprinkle over half Parmesan cheese, then repeat layers. Serve immediately.

CHICKEN LIVER AND VEGETABLE PAN FRY

REALLY EASY!

A great way to use leftover pasta, this dish could be made using any small pasta shapes.

Serves 4

2 tablespoons vegetable oil
1 onion, chopped
1 green pepper, chopped
125g (4 oz) mushrooms, sliced
250g (8 oz) chicken livers, chopped
2 large tomatoes, peeled and chopped
2 fresh sage leaves, chopped
freshly ground black pepper
250g (8 oz) bow pasta, cooked

1 Heat oil in a large frying pan and cook onion for 3-4 minutes or until soft. Add green pepper and cook, stirring, for 3-4 minutes, then add mushrooms and cook for 2 minutes longer.

2 Add chicken livers and cook, stirring, for 3-4 minutes or until livers change colour. Stir in tomatoes, sage and black pepper to taste and cook, stirring constantly, for 4-5 minutes or until juice starts to run from tomatoes.

3 Add pasta to pan and cook for 4-5 minutes longer or until pasta is heated through. Serve immediately.

CHICKEN AND MANGETOUT WITH PASTA

REALLY EASY!

A speedy stir-fry of pasta, cooked chicken, mangetout, chilli and a sherry and soy sauce.

Serves 4

500g (1 lb) wholemeal spiral pasta
2 tablespoons vegetable oil
150g (5 oz) mangetout, trimmed
1 clove garlic, crushed
1 small fresh red chilli, finely chopped
250g (8 oz) chopped cooked chicken
1 tablespoon cornflour, blended with 3 tablespoons
chicken stock
2 tablespoons soy sauce
3 tablespoons dry sherry

1 Bring a large saucepan of water to the boil and cook pasta, following the packet instructions. Drain and set aside.

2 Heat oil in a frying pan or wok. Add mangetout, garlic and chilli and stir-fry for 1 minute. Add chicken and stir-fry for 2 minutes. Toss in cooked pasta, blended cornflour, soy sauce and sherry. Heat through, stirring constantly until the sauce boils and thickens. Serve immediately.

CHICKEN LIVER AND VEGETABLE PAN FRY • CHICKEN AND MANGETOUT

CHICKEN CANNELLONI

EASY!

**Lasagne filled with chicken , bacon and cheese,
rolled up and baked in the oven with
a cream sauce.**

Serves 4

8 sheets fresh lasagne
30g (1 oz) butter
500g (1 lb) fresh chicken mince
180g (6 oz) chicken livers, cleaned and chopped
3 rashers bacon, de-rinded and chopped
100g (3½ oz) grated mozzarella cheese
2 tablespoons grated fresh Parmesan cheese

Cream Sauce

30g (1 oz) butter
1 spring onion, finely chopped
1 clove garlic, crushed
250ml (8 fl oz) double cream
125 ml (4 fl oz) chicken stock
pinch cayenne pepper

1 Cook pasta in boiling water in a large pan for 5 minutes. Drain and place in a bowl of cold water until ready to use.

2 Melt butter in a frying pan over a medium heat, add chicken and cook, stirring, for 5 minutes or until chicken changes colour. Move chicken to one side of pan, add livers and bacon and cook, stirring, for 3-4 minutes longer. Remove pan from heat and set aside to cool.

3 Drain lasagne and pat dry with kitchen paper. Stir mozzarella and Parmesan cheese into chicken mixture. Place heaped spoonfuls of chicken mixture down centre of each lasagne sheet and roll up. Place rolls side by side, seam side down in a greased, shallow ovenproof dish.

Set aside. Preheat oven to 180C,350F,Gas 4.

4 To make sauce, melt butter in a saucepan, add spring onion and garlic and cook, stirring, for 3 minutes. Add cream, stock and cayenne pepper, bring to the boil, then reduce heat and simmer, stirring occasionally, for about 8 minutes or until sauce thickens slightly.

5 Pour sauce over rolls, cover and bake for 20 minutes or until heated through.

CHICKEN CANNELLONI

35

CHICKEN AND PASTA TOSS

REALLY EASY!

Shell pasta tossed with onion, chicken, spinach and pine kernels.

Serves 4

500g (1 lb) shell pasta
30g (1 oz) butter
1 onion, finely chopped
1 clove garlic, crushed
250g (8 oz) cooked chicken, shredded
125 ml (4 fl oz) chicken stock
6 spinach leaves, shredded
freshly ground black pepper
60g (2 oz) pine kernels, toasted

1 Cook pasta in boiling water in a large saucepan, following packet instructions. Drain, set aside and keep warm.

2 Melt butter in a large frying pan and cook onion and garlic, stirring, over a medium heat for 3-4 minutes. Add chicken and stock, and cook for 4-5 minutes longer.

3 Add spinach and pasta to pan, season to taste with black pepper and toss to combine. Sprinkle with pine kernels and serve at once.

PASTA WITH FISH

Pasta and fish make ideal partners in recipes as they both take little time to cook. Canned fish such as tuna goes especially well with pasta and you will find many recipes here that are quick, substantial and extremely tasty.

SEAFOOD CANNELLONI WITH SAFFRON SAUCE

EASY!

Fish and scallops mixed with ricotta cheese, spooned onto lasagne sheets, rolled up and baked with a creamy Saffron Sauce.

Serves 4
8 lasagne sheets, blanched, (or oven-ready) 13 x 16 cm (5 x 6½ inches) cooked size

Filling
30g (1 oz) butter
300g (10 oz) firm-fleshed fish fillets, cut into bite-size pieces
250g (8 oz) scallops, cut into bite-size pieces
ground white pepper
fresh lemon juice
300g (10 oz) ricotta cheese, drained
1 egg, lightly beaten
1 teaspoon finely chopped fresh parsley
1 teaspoon snipped fresh chives
ground (or freshly grated) nutmeg

Saffron Sauce
30g (1 oz) butter
1 tablespoon finely chopped onion
1 clove garlic, crushed
1-2 x 1g sachets pure saffron powder
300 ml (10 fl oz) single cream
ground white pepper

1 To make filling, melt butter in a saucepan and cook fish and scallops for 4-5 minutes or until just opaque. Season to taste with white pepper and lemon juice.

Transfer to a bowl using a slotted spoon. Pour off pan juices and reserve. Place seafood mixture, ricotta cheese, egg, parsley and chives in a bowl. Season to taste with nutmeg. Mix to combine.

2 To make sauce, melt butter in a pan and cook onion and garlic for 4-5 minutes. Add saffron to taste and cook for 1 minute, then pour in cream and reserved seafood juices and season to taste with white pepper. Bring to the boil. Reduce heat and simmer, stirring occasionally, for 5 minutes or until sauce thickens slightly. Strain and discard any solids.

3 Preheat oven to 180C,350F,Gas 4. To make cannelloni, place some filling down the centre of each pasta sheet. Roll up to form a thick tube. Arrange cannelloni in a greased ovenproof dish, pour sauce over and cover with foil. Bake in oven for 20 minutes or until heated through. Serve immediately.

SEAFOOD CANNELLONI WITH SAFFRON SAUCE

SPAGHETTI WITH TUNA AND CRESS

REALLY EASY!

The tuna in this dish is not cooked before adding to the pasta, however, you will find that because it is thinly sliced the heat of the pasta will cook it. Drained canned tuna can be used if you wish.

Serves 4

500g (1 lb) spaghetti
500g (1 lb) fresh tuna steaks, cut into paper thin slices
250g (8 oz) watercress, leaves removed and stems discarded
125g (4 oz) black olives
1 tablespoon finely grated lime rind
2 teaspoons finely grated fresh ginger
60 ml (2 fl oz) balsamic or red wine vinegar
1 tablespoon olive oil
2 tablespoons lime juice

1 Cook pasta in boiling water in a large saucepan of boiling water, following packet directions. Drain well and place in a large serving bowl.

2 Add tuna, watercress, olives, lime rind, ginger, vinegar, oil and lime juice to hot pasta and toss to combine. Serve immediately.

SMOKED SALMON FETTUCCINE

REALLY EASY!

A wonderful combination of pasta, smoked salmon and peas – very quick to make but very special to eat.

Serves 4-6
500g (1 lb) fettuccine

Smoked Salmon Sauce
125g (4 oz) fresh or frozen peas
60 ml (2 fl oz) white wine
300 ml (10 fl oz) double cream
8 slices smoked salmon
3 spring onions, finely chopped
freshly ground black pepper

1 Cook fettuccine in boiling water in a large saucepan, following packet directions. Drain, set aside and keep warm.

2 To make sauce, blanch peas in boiling water for 2 minutes. Refresh under cold running water, drain and set aside. Place wine in a large frying pan and bring to the boil. Stir in 250 ml (8 fl oz) cream and boil until sauce reduces and thickens. Place 4 slices smoked salmon, spring onions and remaining cream in a food processor and purée. Stir smoked salmon mixture into sauce and cook until sauce is hot.

3 Cut remaining salmon slices into strips. Add salmon strips and peas to sauce and season to taste with black pepper. Spoon sauce over fettuccine and toss to combine. Serve immediately.

CURRIED TUNA LASAGNE

EASY!

**A lasagne made with tuna, celery and onion,
topped with a curry sauce.**

Serves 6

*9 sheets instant (oven-ready) lasagne
400g (14 oz) canned tuna, drained and flaked
15g (½ oz) butter
2 stalks celery, finely chopped
1 onion, chopped*

Sauce

*30g (1 oz) butter
4 tablespoons plain flour
2 teaspoons curry powder
560 ml (18 fl oz) milk
180 ml (6 fl oz) water
2 eggs, beaten
2 tablespoons grated Cheddar cheese*

Topping

*2 tablespoons grated Cheddar cheese
1 teaspoon curry powder
½ teaspoon paprika*

1 Preheat oven to 190C, 375F, Gas 5. To make sauce, melt butter in a saucepan. Stir in flour and curry powder and cook for 2-3 minutes. Remove from heat, whisk in combined milk and water. Stir over heat until sauce boils and thickens. Blend in eggs and cheese.

2 Spoon a little sauce over the base of a shallow oven-proof dish. Top with three lasagne sheets and spread over half the tuna.

3 Melt butter in a frying pan and cook celery and onion until soft. Spread half over tuna, top with a layer of sauce.

Repeat layers, finishing with pasta then sauce.

4 To make topping, combine cheese, curry powder and paprika. Sprinkle over top and bake in the oven for 30-35 minutes.

SEAFOOD LASAGNE

EASY!

Lasagne is a great dish when you need to feed a crowd. This recipe can easily be increased to serve 8; simply use a slightly larger dish and a little more seafood. Accompany with a tossed green salad or a sauté of mixed vegetables for a complete meal.

Serves 6

2 tablespoons olive oil
1 leek, white part only, sliced
400g (14 oz) canned tomatoes, undrained and mashed
2 tablespoons tomato purée
500g (1 lb) uncooked prawns, peeled, deveined and chopped
250g (8 oz) firm white fish fillets, cut into pieces
freshly ground black pepper
15 spinach lasagne sheets
90g (3 oz) grated mozzarella cheese

1 Heat oil in a large frying pan and cook leek over a medium heat for 5 minutes or until it softens. Stir in tomatoes and tomato purée and bring to the boil. Reduce heat and simmer, uncovered, for 15 minutes or until sauce reduces and thickens slightly.

2 Add prawns and fish, cover and cook for 3-4 minutes longer. Season to taste with black pepper.

3 Cook lasagne in boiling water in a large saucepan, following packet directions. Drain and place in a bowl of cold water. Preheat oven to 180C,350F,Gas 4.

4 Just prior to assembling, drain lasagne sheets. Spread one-third of the sauce over the base of a deep-sided ovenproof dish and top with half the lasagne sheets. Repeat layers, ending with a layer of sauce. Sprinkle with cheese and bake for 40 minutes.

SPAGHETTI MARINARA

E A S Y !

Spaghetti with tomatoes, basil, wine and mixed seafood.

Serves 4

500g (1 lb) spaghetti
2 teaspoons vegetable oil
2 teaspoons butter
2 onions, chopped
2 x 400g (14 oz) canned tomatoes, undrained and mashed
2 tablespoons chopped fresh basil or 1 teaspoon dried basil
60 ml (2 fl oz) dry white wine
12 mussels, scrubbed and beards removed
12 scallops
12 uncooked prawns, shelled and deveined
125g (4 oz) squid rings

1 Cook pasta in boiling water in a large saucepan, following packet directions. Drain, set aside and keep warm.

2 Heat oil and butter in a frying pan over a medium heat. Add onions and cook, stirring, for 4 minutes or until onions are golden.

3 Stir in tomatoes, basil and wine, bring to a gentle boil and simmer for 8 minutes. Add mussels, scallops and prawns and cook for 2 minutes longer.

4 Add squid and cook for 1 minute or until shellfish is cooked. Spoon shellfish mixture over hot pasta and serve immediately.

SEAFOOD LASAGNE • SPAGHETTI MARINARA

SEAFOOD FETTUCCINE

EASY!

A colourful dish of flavoured fettuccine, red pepper, tomatoes, chilli, spices and seafood.

Serves 4
500g (1 lb) mixed coloured fettuccine

Spicy Seafood Sauce
1 tablespoon olive oil
1 onion, sliced
1 red pepper, diced
1 clove garlic, crushed
1 red chilli, de-seeded and finely chopped
½ teaspoon ground cumin
½ teaspoon ground coriander
400g (14 oz) canned tomatoes, undrained and mashed
60 ml (2 fl oz) dry white wine
1 tablespoon tomato purée
150g (5 oz) squid, cut into rings
150g (5 oz) cleaned fresh mussels in shells
500g (1 lb) uncooked large prawns, peeled and deveined
4 tablespoons finely chopped fresh coriander
freshly ground black pepper

1 To make sauce, heat oil in a large saucepan and cook onion, red pepper, garlic, chilli, cumin and ground coriander for 3-4 minutes or until onion is soft. Add tomatoes, wine and tomato purée and cook over a medium heat for 30 minutes longer or until sauce reduces and thickens.

2 Add squid to sauce and cook for 5 minutes or until just tender. Add mussels and prawns and cook for 4-5 minutes longer. Mix in 2 tablespoons fresh coriander. Season to taste with black pepper.

3 Cook fettuccine in boiling water in a large saucepan, following packet directions. Drain, then spoon sauce over fettuccine and sprinkle with remaining fresh coriander. Serve immediately.

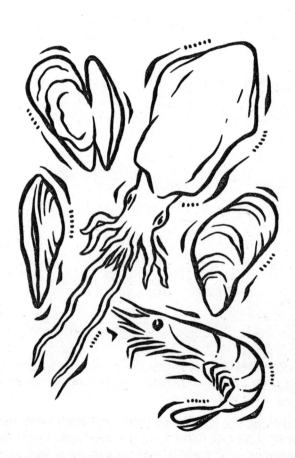

SCALLOP AND RED PEPPER PASTA

EASY!

Fine spaghetti with scallops and prosciutto, mixed with red pepper and leeks and topped with a mixture of garlic, parsley and lemon rind.

Serves 4

500g (1 lb) tagliarini or thin spaghetti
1 tablespoon olive oil
500g (1 lb) prepared scallops
100g (3½ oz) prosciutto or lean ham, cut into thin strips
2 tablespoons lemon juice
2 tablespoons chopped fresh basil or 1 teaspoon dried basil
freshly ground black pepper
250 ml (8 fl oz) chicken stock
1 red pepper, cut into strips
2 leeks, cut into strips

Gremolata

3 cloves garlic, crushed
2 tablespoons finely chopped flat-leaf parsley
1 tablespoon finely grated lemon rind

1 To make Gremolata, place garlic, parsley and lemon rind in a bowl and mix well to combine.

2 Cook pasta in boiling water in a large saucepan, following packet directions. Drain, set aside and keep warm.

3 Heat oil in a frying pan over a medium heat. Add scallops and prosciutto or ham and cook, stirring, for 3 minutes or until scallops just turn opaque and prosciutto or ham is crisp. Remove pan from heat, stir in lemon juice, basil and black pepper to taste and set aside.

4 Place stock in a saucepan, bring to a gentle boil and simmer until reduced by half. Add red pepper and leeks and simmer for 3 minutes. Add pasta and scallop mixture to stock mixture. Toss to combine and top with Gremolata.

BAKED PENNE AND FRESH TUNA

EASY!

Partially cooked pasta, mixed with courgettes, tuna and a cheese sauce and then baked in the oven. If fresh tuna is unavailable, any firm-fleshed fish may be used instead.

Serves 4
350g (12 oz) dried penne, or other short pasta

Tuna Sauce
2 courgettes, sliced
salt
200g (7 oz) butter
350g (12 oz) fresh tuna, cut into chunks
1-2 tablespoons plain flour
250 ml (8 fl oz) milk
freshly ground black pepper
ground (or freshly grated) nutmeg
200g (7 oz) grated fresh Parmesan cheese
150g (5 oz) grated mozzarella cheese

1 To make sauce, sprinkle courgettes with salt and place in a colander or sieve. Set aside to drain for 30 minutes. Rinse and pat dry with absorbent kitchen paper. Melt 30g (1 oz) butter in a frying pan and cook courgettes and tuna until flesh turns white. Remove courgettes and tuna from pan and set aside. Reserve pan juices.

2 Melt 30g (1 oz) butter in a saucepan, add flour and cook for 1-2 minutes. Remove from heat and gradually blend in reserved pan juices and milk. Cook over a medium heat, stirring constantly, until sauce boils and thickens. Season to taste with black pepper and nutmeg. Stir in half the Parmesan cheese and the courgettes and tuna.

3 Cook pasta in boiling water in a large saucepan for half the time stated on packet. Drain and stir into sauce.

4 Preheat oven to 220C,425F,Gas 7. Place one-third pasta mixture in a greased ovenproof dish. Cover with one-third remaining Parmesan and one-third mozzarella. Dot with one third remaining butter. Repeat with remaining pasta mixture, cheese and butter, finishing with butter. Grind black pepper across top and bake in oven for 20 minutes.

BAKED PENNE AND FRESH TUNA

TAGLIATELLE WITH TUNA

REALLY EASY!

**Spaghetti cooked and then topped with a tuna,
wine and tomato sauce.**

Serves 4
350g (12 oz) dried wholemeal tagliatelle or spaghetti

Tuna Sauce
1 onion, finely chopped
1 clove garlic, crushed
400g (14 oz) canned tomatoes, undrained and mashed
1 tablespoon tomato purée
1 tablespoon dry red wine
2 courgettes, sliced
*400g (14 oz) canned tuna in spring water or brine,
drained and flaked*
1 tablespoon finely shredded fresh basil
freshly ground black pepper

1 Cook pasta in boiling water in a large saucepan, following packet directions. Drain, set aside and keep warm.

2 To make sauce, heat a non-stick frying pan and cook onion, garlic and 1 tablespoon of juice from tomatoes for 4-5 minutes or until onion is soft. Stir in tomatoes, tomato purée, wine and courgettes and cook over a low heat for 5 minutes.

3 Add tuna, basil and black pepper to taste to pan and cook for 5 minutes longer or until heated through. To serve, place pasta on serving plates and spoon sauce over.

SPAGHETTI WITH SALMON AND OLIVES

REALLY EASY!

Serves 4

500g (1 lb) spaghetti

Salmon Sauce
400g (14 oz) canned salmon in oil, drained and oil reserved
1 large onion, chopped
1 green pepper, sliced
1 teaspoon minced garlic
350g (12 oz) tomato passata
125 ml (4 fl oz) white wine
1 tablespoon ground black pepper
2 tablespoons finely chopped fresh parsley
8 pitted black olives, halved

1 Cook spaghetti in boiling water in a large saucepan, following packet directions. Drain and set aside to keep warm.

2 To make sauce, heat reserved oil from salmon in a frying pan and cook onion, pepper and garlic for 3-4 minutes or until onion is soft. Stir in tomato passata, and wine and cook for 3-4 minutes.

3 Add salmon to sauce and cook, stirring gently, for 4-5 minutes. Spoon sauce over spaghetti and toss to combine. Garnish with black pepper, parsley and olives.

TAGLIATELLE WITH TUNA • SPAGHETTI WITH SALMON AND OLIVES

PASTA WITH MEAT

Over recent years pasta has changed from being regarded as humble 'peasant' food, to something that is modern, healthy and fashionable to eat. With many people choosing to eat less meat, for various reasons, pasta dishes have become very popular. The amount of meat needed to make a very filling pasta dish, is much less than that needed if meat was served alone. Our busy lifestyles also mean that dishes that are quick, all in one meals, are the ones we like to cook. You will find here popular dishes such as Lasagne and Spaghetti Bolognese, but do try some of the new ideas such as Pork and Macaroni Pie and Tortellini with Onion Confit.

SPAGHETTI BOLOGNESE

REALLY EASY!

For an easy family meal serve this all-time favourite with steamed vegetables or a tossed green salad and crusty bread or rolls.

Serves 4
500g (1 lb) spaghetti
grated Parmesan cheese (optional)

Bolognese Sauce
2 teaspoons vegetable oil
1 clove garlic, crushed
1 onion, chopped
500g (1 lb) beef mince
400g (14 oz) tomato passata
60 ml (2 fl oz) red wine or water
1 tablespoon chopped fresh oregano or ½ teaspoon dried oregano
1 tablespoon chopped fresh thyme or ½ teaspoon dried thyme
freshly ground black pepper

1 To make sauce, heat oil in a frying pan over a medium heat. Add garlic and onion and cook, stirring, for 3 minutes or until onion is soft.

2 Add beef and cook, stirring, for 5 minutes or until meat is well browned. Stir in tomato passata, wine or water, oregano and thyme. Bring to a gentle boil and simmer, stirring occasionally, for 15 minutes or until sauce reduces and thickens. Season to taste with black pepper.

3 Cook pasta in boiling water in a large saucepan, following packet directions. Drain well. To serve, spoon sauce over hot pasta and top with Parmesan cheese, if using.

TRADITIONAL LASAGNE

EASY!

Lasagne is delicious served with a salad of lightly cooked, warm, mixed vegetables tossed with an Italian dressing.

Serves 6

12-18 sheets instant (oven-ready) lasagne
60g (2 oz) grated mozzarella cheese

Cheese Sauce
75g (2½ oz) butter
45g (1½ oz) flour
500 ml (16 fl oz) milk
90g (3 oz) grated mature Cheddar cheese
freshly ground black pepper

Meat Sauce
2 teaspoons vegetable oil
2 onions, chopped
2 cloves garlic, crushed
750g (1½ lb) beef mince
400g (14 oz) canned tomatoes, undrained and mashed
180 ml (6 fl oz) red wine
2 tablespoons chopped mixed herbs

1 To make Cheese Sauce, melt butter in a saucepan over a medium heat. Stir in flour and cook, stirring, for 1 minute. Remove pan from heat and whisk in milk. Return pan to heat and cook, stirring, for 4-5 minutes or until sauce boils and thickens. Stir in cheese and black pepper to taste and set aside.

2 To make Meat Sauce, heat oil in a frying pan over a medium heat. Add onions and garlic and cook, stirring, for 3 minutes or until onions are soft. Add beef and cook, stirring, for 5 minutes or until beef is brown. Stir in tomatoes, wine and herbs, bring to a gentle boil and simmer, stirring occasionally, for 15 minutes or until sauce reduces and thickens. Season to taste with black pepper.

3 Preheat the oven to 180C,350F,Gas 4. Line the base of a large, greased baking dish with a third of the lasagne sheets. Top with one-half of the Meat Sauce and one-third of the Cheese Sauce. Repeat layers to use all ingredients, ending with a layer of Cheese Sauce.

4 Sprinkle top of lasagne with mozzarella cheese and bake for 30-40 minutes or until hot and bubbling and top is golden.

TRADITIONAL LASAGNE

LAMB LASAGNE WITH SPINACH AND CHEESE

EASY!

As an accompaniment to this substantial lasagne choose something light, such as a tomato and herb salad.

Serves 6
9 sheets instant (oven-ready) lasagne
60g (2 oz) grated mature Cheddar cheese
2 tablespoons grated Parmesan cheese

Meat Sauce
2 teaspoons olive oil
1 onion, chopped
2 cloves garlic, crushed
2 rashers bacon, chopped
125g (4 oz) button mushrooms, sliced
500g (1 lb) lean lamb mince
400g (14 oz) canned tomatoes, undrained and mashed
125 ml (4 fl oz) red wine
½ teaspoon dried basil
½ teaspoon dried oregano
1 teaspoon sugar

Spinach Cheese Sauce
30g (1 oz) butter
2 tablespoons flour
250 ml (8 fl oz) milk
125 ml (4 fl oz) single cream
60g (2 oz) grated mature Cheddar cheese
250g (8 oz) frozen spinach, thawed and drained
freshly ground black pepper

1 To make Meat Sauce, heat oil in a large frying pan

and cook onion, garlic, bacon and mushrooms over a medium heat for 4-5 minutes or until onion is soft.

2 Add lamb to pan and cook, stirring to break up meat, for 4-5 minutes or until meat is brown. Combine tomatoes, wine, basil, oregano and sugar, and pour into pan with meat mixture. Bring to the boil, then reduce heat, cover and simmer for 35 minutes or until sauce thickens.

3 To make Spinach Cheese Sauce, melt butter in a saucepan and cook flour for 1-2 minutes. Remove pan from heat and stir in milk and cream. Cook, stirring constantly, over a medium heat for 4-5 minutes or until sauce boils and thickens. Remove pan from heat and stir in cheese and spinach. Season to taste with black pepper.

4 Preheat oven to 190C,375F,Gas 5. To assemble lasagne, spread one-third of the Spinach Cheese Sauce over base of a lightly greased, shallow 28 x 18 cm (11 x 7 inch) ovenproof dish. Top with three lasagne sheets, spread half the Meat Sauce over, then another third of the Spinach Cheese Sauce. Top with another three lasagne sheets and remaining Meat Sauce. Place remaining lasagne sheets over Meat Sauce and top with remaining Spinach Cheese Sauce.

5 Combine Cheddar cheese and Parmesan cheese and sprinkle over lasagne and bake for 40 minutes or until top is golden.

LAMB LASAGNE WITH SPINACH AND CHEESE

SPIRELLI WITH HAM AND ARTICHOKES

REALLY EASY!

Quickly cooked pasta with ham, artichoke hearts, eggs and cheese.

Serves 4

500g (1 lb) fresh spirelli
2 teaspoons olive oil
300g (10 oz) ham, cut into strips
6 canned artichoke hearts, sliced length ways
3 eggs, beaten with 1 tablespoon grated fresh Parmesan cheese
freshly ground black pepper

1 Cook spirelli in boiling water in a large saucepan, following packet directions or until 'al dente'. Drain, set aside and keep warm.

2 Heat oil in a frying pan and cook ham and artichoke hearts for 1-2 minutes.

3 Add pasta and toss to combine Remove from heat and quickly stir in egg mixture. Season to taste with black pepper. Serve as soon as the eggs start to stick to spirelli – this will take only a few seconds

MACARONI CHEESE AND SPICY SAUSAGE

EASY!

Macaroni with spicy sausage, shallots, mushrooms and red pepper in a creamy sauce.

Serves 4

30g (1 oz) butter
4 shallots, chopped
½ red pepper, finely chopped
125g (4 oz) mushrooms, sliced
350g (12 oz) cooked spicy sausage, sliced
500g (1 lb) cooked macaroni

Sauce

60g (2 oz) butter
3 tablespoons plain flour
300 ml (10 fl oz) milk
1 teaspoon French mustard
3 tablespoons single cream or evaporated milk
3 tablespoons grated Parmesan cheese
125g (4 oz) grated Cheddar cheese
paprika

1 Preheat oven to 200C,400F,Gas 6. Place butter, shallots, pepper, mushrooms and sausage slices in a saucepan. Cook for 2-3 minutes, remove and set aside.

2 To make sauce, melt butter in pan, add flour and cook for 1 minute. Pour in combined milk, mustard and cream. Cook, for 3-4 minutes, stirring all the time, until sauce boils and thickens. Mix in Parmesan cheese.

3 Combine macaroni, mushroom mixture and sauce. Spoon into a lightly greased, shallow, ovenproof dish, top with cheese and dust lightly with paprika. Bake in oven for 10 minutes until cheese melts.

CHEESY MEATBALLS WITH SPAGHETTI

EASY!

A great family dish of spaghetti topped with Cheesy Meatballs and Tomato Sauce.

Serves 4
250g (8 oz) spaghetti

Cheesy Meatballs
500g (1 lb) lean beef mince
2 tablespoons finely chopped fresh parsley
60g (2 oz) grated Parmesan cheese
2 teaspoons tomato purée
1 egg, beaten

Tomato Sauce
15g (½ oz) butter
1 onion, finely chopped
2 teaspoons dried basil
1 teaspoon dried oregano
400g (14 oz) canned tomatoes, undrained and mashed
2 tablespoons tomato purée
125 ml (4 fl oz) beef stock
125 ml (4 fl oz) white wine
1 teaspoon caster sugar
freshly ground black pepper

1 To make meatballs, place beef, parsley, Parmesan cheese, tomato purée and egg in a bowl, and mix to combine. Form mixture into small balls and cook in a non-stick frying pan for 4-5 minutes or until brown. Remove meatballs from pan and drain on absorbent kitchen paper.

2 To make sauce, melt butter in a large frying pan and

cook onion, basil and oregano for 2-3 minutes or until onion is soft. Stir in tomatoes, tomato purée, beef stock, wine and sugar. Bring to the boil, then reduce heat and simmer, stirring occasionally, for 30 minutes or until sauce reduces and thickens. Season to taste with black pepper. Add meatballs to sauce and cook for 5 minutes longer.

3 Cook spaghetti in boiling water in a large saucepan, following packet directions. Drain, place in a warm serving bowl and top with meatballs and sauce. Serve immediately.

CHEESY MEATBALLS WITH SPAGHETTI

FETTUCCINE WITH VEAL CREAM SAUCE

REALLY EASY!

Fettuccine with a saucy topping of veal strips with parsley, paprika, brandy, tomato purée and sour cream.

Serves 4
500g (1 lb) fresh fettuccine
1 tablespoon olive oil
500g (1 lb) thin veal steaks, cut into strips
1 clove garlic, crushed
1 teaspoon chopped fresh parsley
2 teaspoons paprika
1½ tablespoons brandy
2 tablespoons tomato purée
400g (14 oz) thick sour cream
freshly ground black pepper

1 Cook fettuccine in boiling water in a large saucepan until 'al dente'. Drain, set aside and keep warm.

2 Heat oil in a large frying pan and cook veal for 3-4 minutes or until browned. Add garlic, parsley and paprika and cook for 1- 2 minutes longer. Stir in brandy and cook until evaporated. Whisk in tomato purée and sour cream. Season to taste with black pepper and bring to the boil. Reduce heat and simmer until sauce reduces and thickens. Stir in pasta and toss to coat.

PEPPERONI TOSS

REALLY EASY!

Cooked spaghetti tossed with onion, olives and pepperoni slices.

Serves 4

350g (12 oz) spaghetti
2 tablespoons olive oil
1 onion, finely chopped
90g (3 oz) stoned black olives, chopped
180g (6 oz) pepperoni salami, chopped

1 Cook spaghetti in boiling water in a large saucepan, following packet directions. Drain, set aside and keep warm.

2 Heat oil in a large frying pan and cook onion over a medium heat for 5-6 minutes or until onion is transparent. Add olives and salami and cook for 2 minutes longer.

3 Add spaghetti to pan and toss to combine. Serve immediately.

FETTUCCINE WITH VEAL CREAM SAUCE • PEPPERONI TOSS

TORTELLINI WITH RED PEPPER SAUCE

REALLY EASY!

Canned sweet red peppers are available from Continental delicatessens and some supermarkets. They are sometimes called pimentos. You may wish to use fresh red peppers instead of the canned ones. You will require 4 large peppers for this recipe and they need to be roasted and the skin removed before making the sauce.

Serves 4
500g (1 lb) meat-filled tortellini

Red Pepper Sauce
1 tablespoon vegetable oil
1 onion, chopped
400g (14 oz) canned sweet red peppers, drained and chopped
250 ml (8 fl oz) water
1 tablespoon honey
1 tablespoon chopped fresh oregano
freshly ground black pepper

1 Cook tortellini in boiling water in a large saucepan, following packet directions. Drain, set aside and keep warm.

2 To make sauce, heat oil in a small frying pan and cook onion, stirring, for 3 minutes or until onion is soft. Place red peppers, water, honey, oregano and onion in a food processor or blender and process to make a smooth sauce.

3 Pour pepper sauce into a large saucepan and heat over a medium heat for 4-5 minutes or until sauce is simmering. Season to taste with black pepper. Spoon sauce over tortellini and toss to combine.

TORTELLINI WITH PARSLEY BUTTER

REALLY EASY!

There is a legend that says tortellini was created to honour Venus' bellybutton. Apparently, an innkeeper in Bologna was so inflamed with this beautiful young woman that, after showing her to her room, he then spied on her through the keyhole as she was undressing; but all he could see was her bellybutton. He rushed to his kitchen and created tortellini as a memento to Venus' beauty.

Serves 4
500g (1 lb) meat-filled tortellini
2 tablespoons olive oil
125g (4 oz) grated fresh Parmesan cheese
125g (4 oz) butter, cut into small cubes
pinch nutmeg
30g (1 oz) chopped fresh parsley
freshly ground black pepper

1 Place tortellini and olive oil in a large saucepan of boiling water and cook, following packet directions. Drain and place in a large serving bowl.

2 Top tortellini with Parmesan cheese, butter, nutmeg, parsley and black pepper to taste. Toss to combine and serve immediately.

SPAGHETTI CARBONARA

REALLY EASY!

Spaghetti tossed in a creamy sauce of ham, cheese, eggs and cream.

Serves 4

180g (6 oz) sliced ham, cut into strips
4 eggs
90 ml (3 fl oz) single cream
90g (3 oz) grated fresh Parmesan cheese
500g (1 lb) spaghetti
freshly ground black pepper

1 Cook ham in a non-stick frying pan for 2-3 minutes. Place eggs, cream and Parmesan cheese in a bowl and beat lightly to combine.

2 Cook spaghetti in boiling water in a large saucepan, following packet directions. Drain spaghetti, add egg mixture and ham and toss so that the heat of the spaghetti cooks the sauce. Season to taste with black pepper and serve immediately.

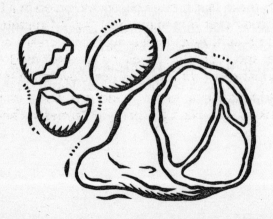

FETTUCCINE WITH BACON AND AVOCADO

REALLY EASY!

An unusual but delicious dish of fettuccine with a Bacon and Avocado Sauce.

Serves 4
350g (12 oz) fettuccine

Bacon and Avocado Sauce
6 rashers back bacon, trimmed and chopped
1 red onion, sliced
2 avocados, peeled, stones removed and flesh puréed
2 tablespoons cream
2 tablespoons lemon juice
freshly ground black pepper
3 tablespoons grated Parmesan cheese

1 Cook fettuccine in boiling water in a large saucepan, following packet directions. Drain and set aside to keep warm.

2 To make sauce, place bacon and onion in a frying pan and cook over a medium heat for 3-4 minutes or until onion is soft. Add puréed avocados, cream and lemon juice, and cook, stirring, over a low heat for 3-4 minutes or until heated through. Do not allow sauce to boil.

3 Add fettuccine to sauce and toss. Serve immediately, sprinkled with black pepper and Parmesan cheese.

SPAGHETTI CARBONARA • FETTUCCINE WITH BACON AND AVOCADO

TORTELLINI WITH ONION CONFIT

EASY!

Meat-filled tortellini in a sauce of reduced stock with peas and an onion confit made with onions, red wine and thyme.

Serves 4

375ml (12 fl oz) beef stock
750g (1½ oz) beef or veal tortellini
250g (8 oz) frozen petit pois
2 tablespoons chopped fresh tarragon

Onion Confit

30g (1 oz) butter
2 onions, thinly sliced
2 teaspoons sugar
1 tablespoon chopped fresh thyme or ½ teaspoon dried thyme
250 ml (8 fl oz) red wine
2 tablespoons red wine vinegar

1 To make confit, melt butter in a saucepan over a medium heat, add onions and cook, stirring, for 3 minutes or until onions are soft. Stir in sugar and cook for 2 minutes longer. Add thyme, wine and vinegar, bring to a gentle boil and simmer gently, stirring frequently, for 40 minutes or until mixture reduces and thickens.

2 Place stock in a saucepan, bring to the boil and boil until reduced by half. Keep warm.

3 Cook pasta in boiling water in a large saucepan, following packet instructions. Drain well. Add pasta, confit, peas and tarragon to stock, bring to the boil and simmer for 2-3 minutes or until peas are cooked.

SPAGHETTI WITH SALAMI AND TOMATO SAUCE

REALLY EASY!

Spaghetti with a rich sauce of tomatoes with aubergine, red pepper, courgettes, salami and olives.

Serves 4

1 medium aubergine, cut into 2.5 cm (1 inch) cubes
salt
olive oil
1 small onion, sliced length ways
1 small red pepper, cut into short strips
2 small courgettes, sliced
400g (14 oz) canned tomatoes, undrained and mashed
freshly ground black pepper
180g (6 oz) piece salami, cut into small cubes
500g (1 lb) dried wholemeal spaghetti
8-10 small black olives
grated fresh Parmesan cheese

1 Sprinkle aubergine with salt and place in a colander to drain. Heat a little olive oil in a frying pan and gently cook onion, red pepper and courgettes for 4-5 minutes or until onion softens. Remove from pan and set aside. Rinse aubergine under cold water, then pat dry with kitchen paper. Add a little more olive oil to pan and cook aubergine until golden. Pour off any excess oil and return onion mixture to pan.

2 Add tomatoes and season to taste with black pepper. Cook over a low heat, stirring occasionally, for 10 minutes. Add salami and mix in.

3 Cook spaghetti in a large saucepan of boiling water, following packet instructions. Drain, transfer to a warm serving platter, spoon over hot sauce, then sprinkle with olives and Parmesan cheese.

PORK AND MACARONI PIE

**A cheese pastry flan filled with pork and
mushrooms and topped with macaroni
in a parsley sauce.**

Serves 6
350g (12 oz) prepared shortcrust pastry
60g (2oz) Cheddar cheese

Pork and Mushroom Filling
30g (1 oz) butter
1 onion, chopped
500g (1 lb) lean pork mince
250g (8 oz) tomato passata
125 ml (4 fl oz) dry white wine
250g (8 oz) button mushrooms, sliced

Macaroni Filling
180g (6 oz) macaroni
30g (1oz) butter
2 tablespoons flour
250 ml (8 fl oz) hot milk
1 tablespoon chopped fresh parsley

1 Preheat oven to 200C,400F,Gas 6. Roll out pastry to fit
a deep-sided 23 cm (9 inch) flan dish. Line pastry case
with non-stick baking paper and weigh down with
baking beans or uncooked rice. Bake pastry case for 10-
15 minutes, then remove rice and paper and set pastry
case aside to cool.

2 To make Pork and Mushroom Filling, melt butter in a
large saucepan and cook onion for 2-3 minutes, then
add pork and cook, stirring to break up meat, for 10
minutes longer or until meat changes colour. Stir in
tomato passata, wine and mushrooms. Bring meat

mixture to the boil and simmer, uncovered, for 20 minutes.

3 To make Macaroni Filling, cook macaroni in boiling water in a large saucepan, following packet instructions. Drain and set aside. Melt butter in a saucepan and stir in the flour and cook for 1 minute. Stir in hot milk and cook, stirring constantly, for 4-5 minutes or until sauce thickens. Remove sauce from heat and stir in macaroni and parsley. Season to taste with black pepper.

4 Spread Pork and Mushroom Filling over base of pastry case, top with Macaroni Filling and sprinkle with cheese. Reduce oven temperature to 180C,350F,Gas 4, and bake pie for 25-30 minutes or until top is golden.

PORK AND MACARONI PIE

SAUCES FOR PASTA

Pasta is a wonderful store cupboard ingredient and very often all you need to make a quick, delicious and filling meal is a freshly made sauce. Here you will find your favourite recipes for Tomato, Marinara, Mushroom and many more that are excellent additions to pasta.

MARINARA SAUCE

REALLY EASY!

Serves 4
1 tablespoon olive oil
4 shallots, finely chopped
1 clove garlic, crushed
1 small red chilli, finely chopped
500g (1 lb) cooked prawns, peeled, deveined and chopped
125g (4 oz) scallops, halved, with coral removed
400g (14 oz) canned tomatoes, undrained and mashed
3 tablespoons red wine
3 tablespoons chicken stock
2 teaspoons tomato purée
1 teaspoon sugar
2 teaspoons chopped fresh basil
1 tablespoon chopped fresh parsley
8 oysters in the shell (optional)

1 Heat oil in a large saucepan and cook shallots, garlic and chilli for 1 minute. Stir in prawns and scallops and cook for 2 minutes longer.

2 Combine tomatoes, wine, stock, tomato purée and sugar and pour into pan with prawn mixture. Bring to the boil, then reduce heat and simmer, uncovered, for 10 minutes.

3 Add basil and parsley. Cook for 2-3 minutes. Spoon sauce over hot, cooked pasta. Garnish with oysters in their shells.

TUNA AND OLIVE SAUCE
REALLY EASY!

Serves 4
30g (1 oz) butter
2 tablespoons plain flour
125 ml (4 fl oz) milk
3 tablespoons chicken stock
400g (14 oz) tuna in brine, drained and liquid reserved
1 tablespoon finely chopped fresh dill
12 black olives, pitted and sliced
2 tablespoons capers, finely chopped
2-3 drops Tabasco sauce
3 tablespoons single cream
2 tablespoons lemon juice
freshly ground black pepper

1 Melt butter in a saucepan, add flour and cook for 1 minute. Remove from heat.

2 Blend in milk, stock and tuna liquid, stirring over a medium heat until sauce boils and thickens.

3 Reduce heat and add dill, olives, capers, Tabasco, cream and lemon juice. Season to taste with pepper and stir well to combine.

4 Break up tuna into smaller chunks and fold through sauce. Cook for 2-3 minutes to heat through. Spoon sauce over hot, cooked pasta and serve.

MUSHROOM, BROCCOLI AND BACON SAUCE

REALLY EASY!

Serves 4
1 small head broccoli, cut into small florets
2 teaspoons olive oil
4 bacon rashers, chopped
125g (4 oz) button mushrooms, sliced
1 clove garlic, crushed
300 ml (10 fl oz) single cream
freshly ground black pepper
3 tablespoons finely chopped fresh parsley

1 Boil, steam or microwave broccoli until just tender. Drain and refresh under cold running water. Drain and set aside.

2 Heat oil in a frying pan and cook bacon for 3-4 minutes or until crisp. Stir in mushrooms and garlic and cook for 2-3 minutes.

3 Pour in cream, bring to the boil, stirring frequently, and simmer for 5 minutes or until sauce thickens. Season to taste with pepper, add broccoli and heat through. Spoon sauce over hot, cooked pasta. Sprinkle with parsley and serve.

TUNA AND OLIVE SAUCE • MUSHROOM, BROCCOLI AND BACON SAUCE

YOGURT HERB SAUCE

REALLY EASY!

Serves 4
15g (½ oz) butter
1 small onion, chopped
1 clove garlic, crushed
2 tablespoons flour
125 ml (4 fl oz) vegetable stock
200g (7 oz) natural yogurt
2 tablespoons finely chopped fresh parsley
2 tablespoons finely chopped fresh basil
2 tablespoons snipped fresh chives
freshly ground black pepper

1 To make sauce, melt butter in a saucepan and cook onion and garlic over a medium heat for 2-3 minutes. Stir in flour and stock and cook, stirring constantly, for 4-5 minutes longer or until sauce boils and thickens.

2 Remove pan from heat, stir in yogurt and cook over a low heat for 2-3 minutes longer. Mix in parsley, basil and chives and season to taste with black pepper. Spoon sauce over cooked pasta and serve immediately.

CHICKEN LIVER SAUCE

REALLY EASY!

Serves 4

30g (1 oz) butter
4 rashers bacon, chopped
1 onion, finely chopped
1 clove garlic, crushed
350g (12 oz) chicken livers, chopped
2 teaspoons flour
180 ml (6 fl oz) chicken stock
1 teaspoon tomato purée
1 teaspoon chopped fresh marjoram or ½ teaspoon dried marjoram
freshly ground black pepper
60g (2 oz) sour cream

1 Melt butter in a saucepan and cook bacon, onion and garlic over a medium heat for 4-5 minutes or until onion is soft. Add chicken livers and cook, stirring, for 4-5 minutes or until livers change colour.

2 Stir in flour, then gradually blend in stock. Add tomato purée, marjoram and black pepper to taste. Cover and cook, stirring occasionally, over a low heat for 10 minutes. Just prior to serving, stir in sour cream.

YOGURT HERB SAUCE • CHICKEN LIVER SAUCE

TOMATO SAUCE

REALLY EASY!

Serves 4

1 tablespoon olive oil
1 onion, finely chopped
1 clove garlic, crushed
500g (1 lb) ripe tomatoes, peeled and roughly chopped
1 tablespoon tomato purée
½ teaspoon sugar
1 tablespoon chopped fresh basil
freshly ground black pepper

1 Heat oil in a saucepan and cook onion and garlic over a medium heat for 4-5 minutes or until onion is soft. Add tomatoes, tomato purée, sugar and basil.

2 Bring sauce to a gentle boil, cover and simmer, stirring occasionally, for 30 minutes or until sauce reduces and thickens. Season to taste with black pepper.

TOMATO BOLOGNESE

EASY!

Serves 4

2 tablespoons olive oil
2 rashers bacon, chopped
1 onion, chopped
1 carrot, chopped
1 stalk celery, chopped
1 clove garlic, crushed
250g (8 oz) lean beef mince
125g (4 oz) chicken livers, chopped
2 tablespoons tomato purée
225g (8 oz) can chopped tomatoes, undrained
125 ml (4 fl oz) dry white wine
125 ml (4 fl oz) beef or chicken stock
pinch ground nutmeg
freshly ground black pepper

1 Heat oil in a large saucepan and cook bacon, stirring, over a medium heat for 3-4 minutes. Add onion, carrot, celery and garlic and cook, stirring, for 5 minutes longer or until vegetables start to brown.

2 Add beef mince to pan and cook, stirring to break up meat, for 5-6 minutes or until beef mince browns. Add chicken livers and cook for 2-3 minutes or until livers change colour.

3 Stir in tomato purée, tomatoes, wine, stock and nutmeg. Bring sauce to simmering, cover and simmer for 30-40 minutes or until sauce reduces and thickens. Season to taste with black pepper.

TUNA AND TOMATO SAUCE

REALLY EASY!

Serves 4
1 teaspoon olive oil
1 onion, finely chopped
1 clove garlic, crushed
400g (14 oz) canned tomatoes, undrained and mashed
1 tablespoon tomato purée
1 tablespoon dry red wine
1 teaspoon sugar
400g (14 oz) canned tuna, drained and flaked
1 tablespoon finely chopped fresh parsley
1 tablespoon finely chopped fresh dill
freshly ground black pepper

1 To make sauce, heat oil in a frying pan and cook onion and garlic over a medium heat for 4-5 minutes or until onion is soft. Stir in tomatoes, tomato purée, wine and sugar. Bring to the boil, then add tuna, parsley and dill. Reduce heat and simmer for 10 minutes or until sauce reduces and thickens.

CREAMY ASPARAGUS SAUCE

REALLY EASY!

Serves 4

500g (1 lb) fresh asparagus spears, trimmed
1 tablespoon olive oil
1 thick slice whole grain bread, made into breadcrumbs
250 ml (8 fl oz) evaporated milk
60g (2 oz) grated mozzarella cheese
freshly ground black pepper

1 To make sauce, steam, boil or microwave asparagus until tender. Drain and refresh under cold running water. Cut asparagus into 2.5 cm (1 inch) pieces and set aside.

2 Heat oil in a frying pan and cook breadcrumbs over a low heat, stirring constantly, for 2 minutes. Stir in milk and asparagus, and cook, stirring occasionally, over a medium heat for 5 minutes. Mix in cheese and season to taste with black pepper.

TUNA AND TOMATO SAUCE • CREAMY ASPARAGUS SAUCE

MUSHROOM AND TOMATO SAUCE

REALLY EASY!

Serves 4
60g (2 oz) butter
2 onions, chopped
400g (14 oz) canned tomatoes, undrained and mashed
2 tablespoons tomato purée
125g (4 oz) mushrooms, sliced
4 courgettes, sliced
1 tablespoon chopped fresh oregano or 1 teaspoon dried oregano
2 bay leaves
freshly ground black pepper

1 To make sauce, melt butter in a saucepan and cook onions for 3-4 minutes or until soft. Add tomatoes, tomato purée, mushrooms, courgettes, oregano and bay leaves and bring to the boil. Reduce heat, cover and simmer, stirring occasionally, for 30 minutes or until sauce reduces and thickens. Season to taste with black pepper.

Remove bay leaves before serving.

SPINACH SAUCE

REALLY EASY!

Serves 4
250g (8 oz) spinach, shredded
45g (1½ oz) butter
2 cloves garlic, crushed
375 ml (12 fl oz) double cream
125g (4 oz) grated fresh Parmesan cheese
freshly ground black pepper

1 To make sauce, boil, steam or microwave spinach for 2-3 minutes or until just cooked. Drain and set aside.

2 Melt butter in a saucepan and cook garlic over a low heat for 2 minutes. Stir in cream and Parmesan cheese and cook, stirring constantly, for 2-3 minutes or until smooth. Stir spinach into sauce and season to taste with black pepper.

MUSHROOM AND TOMATO SAUCE • SPINACH SAUCE

THREE-CHEESE SAUCE WITH PISTACHIOS

REALLY EASY!

Serves 4
250 ml (8 fl oz) single cream
90g (3 oz) Gorgonzola, crumbled
75g (2½ oz) grated fresh Parmesan
60g (2 oz) grated Gruyère cheese
60g (2 oz) shelled pistachio nuts, chopped
1 teaspoon finely chopped basil
ground white pepper

1 Put cream into a saucepan and bring slowly to the boil. Reduce heat, add Gorgonzola cheese and stir until melted and smooth. Stir in Parmesan and Gruyère cheeses. Cook over a low heat, stirring constantly, until sauce is thick and smooth.

2 Add the pistachio nuts and basil. Season to taste with pepper. To serve, pour over cooked pasta of your choice.

RICOTTA AND HERB SAUCE

REALLY EASY!

Serves 4
1 egg yolk
150g (5 oz) ricotta cheese
90 ml (3 fl oz) double cream
4 tablespoons grated fresh Parmesan cheese
1 teaspoon finely snipped fresh chives
1 teaspoon finely chopped fresh parsley
coarsely ground white pepper

1 Beat egg yolk into ricotta cheese and mix until smooth. Set aside.

2 Heat cream in a saucepan, stir in Parmesan cheese, chives and parsley. Season to taste with white pepper. Beat in ricotta mixture and heat through gently just before serving on cooked pasta.

THREE-CHEESE SAUCE WITH PISTACHIOS • RICOTTA AND HERB SAUCE

MUSSEL, TOMATO AND ORANGE SAUCE

EASY !

Serves 4

3 x 400g (14 oz) cans tomatoes, drained
1½ tablespoons olive oil
1 onion, chopped
1 clove garlic, crushed
½ teaspoon dried chilli flakes
200ml (7 fl oz) dry white wine
1 tablespoon finely chopped fresh oregano, or 1 teaspoon dried oregano
½ teaspoon sugar
3 tablespoons orange juice
freshly ground black pepper
16 mussels, cleaned and scrubbed
2 teaspoons grated orange rind
2 tablespoons finely chopped fresh parsley

1 Remove the seeds from the tomatoes with a teaspoon and mash the flesh.

2 Heat oil in a large saucepan and cook onion, garlic, and chilli flakes for 5 minutes. Mix in tomatoes, 100 ml (3½ fl oz) wine, oregano, sugar and orange juice. Season to taste with pepper. Bring to the boil, then reduce heat and simmer for 40 minutes, or until sauce reduces and thickens.

3 Preheat oven to 220C,425F,Gas 7. Place mussels in a baking dish and pour in remaining wine. Bake in the oven for 8-10 minutes or until mussels open. Discard any unopened mussels.

4 Combine orange rind and parsley. Toss mussels into sauce and sprinkle with parsley mixture.

ANCHOVY AND GREEN OLIVE SAUCE

REALLY EASY!

Serves 4

150g (5 oz) pitted green olives, sliced
1 teaspoon finely chopped anchovy fillets
60g (2 oz) freshly grated Parmesan cheese
60g (2 oz) walnuts, finely chopped
2 teaspoons chopped fresh oregano
2 teaspoons chopped fresh basil
1 tablespoon chopped fresh parsley
125 ml (4 fl oz) virgin olive oil
freshly ground black pepper

1 Combine olives, anchovy fillets, Parmesan cheese, walnuts, oregano, basil and parsley in a bowl.

2 Gradually mix in olive oil, until a thin paste is formed. Stand for 1 hour. Season with black pepper. Store in the fridge for up to five days. To use, spoon over hot pasta and toss well.

SALADS

Cooked pasta makes a marvellous addition to salads. It provides a lovely contrast to crisp vegetables, spicy or creamy dressings, and pasta salads are ideal for summer meals, picnics, barbecues and parties. Pasta for salads should be cooked until firm but not too soft, and then immediately drained and rinsed under cold running water until completely cold. This stops the pasta from sticking together. It is usually best to serve pasta salads at room temperature for maximum flavour.

TORTELLINI SALAD

REALLY EASY!

Cooked tortellini with asparagus, mangetout, tomatoes, lettuce and red pepper, coated in French dressing.

Serves 4
750g (1½ lb) meat-filled tortellini
250g (8 oz) asparagus, cut into 5 cm (2 inch) pieces
200g (7 oz) mangetout, trimmed
1 lettuce
1 red pepper, sliced
250g (8 oz) cherry tomatoes
125 ml (4 fl oz) French dressing

1 Cook tortellini in boiling water in a large saucepan, following packet directions. Drain, rinse under cold water and set aside to cool.

2 Boil, steam or microwave asparagus and mangetout separately until tender. Refresh under cold running water and set aside to cool.

3 Arrange lettuce, red pepper, tomatoes, tortellini, asparagus and mangetout in large serving bowl. Pour dressing over and serve immediately.

SEAFOOD AND DILL SALAD

EASY!

**Pieces of white fish with fettucine, tender sticks
of courgette, carrot and celery, tossed in
a Dill Dressing.**

Serves 6

*750g (1½ lb) firm white fish fillets, lightly cooked, cooled
and cut into 2.5 cm (1 inch) cubes*
2 tablespoons lemon juice
2 tablespoons finely chopped fresh dill
pinch cayenne pepper
freshly ground black pepper
125g (4 oz) spinach fettuccine
125g (4 oz) tomato fettuccine
125g (4 oz) plain fettuccine
3 courgettes, cut into matchsticks
2 carrots, cut into matchsticks
2 sticks celery, cut into matchsticks

Dill Dressing

1 teaspoon Dijon mustard
2 tablespoons finely chopped fresh dill
2 tablespoons lemon juice
4 tablespoons vegetable oil
freshly ground black pepper

1 Place fish, lemon juice, dill, cayenne pepper and black
pepper to taste in a bowl. Toss to combine and set aside
to marinate for 40 minutes.

2 Cook spinach, tomato and plain fettuccine together in
boiling water in a large saucepan, following packet directions. Drain, rinse under cold running water, then drain
again and set aside to cool completely.

3 Steam or microwave courgettes, carrots and celery
separately for 2-3 minutes or until just tender. Refresh

under cold running water and set aside to cool completely.

4 Drain fish and place fish, fettuccine, courgettes, carrots and celery in a large salad bowl.

5 To make dressing, place mustard, dill, lemon juice, oil and black pepper to taste in a screw top jar and shake to combine. Pour dressing over salad and toss gently. Serve immediately.

SEAFOOD AND DILL SALAD

PASTA AND FETA SALAD

REALLY EASY!

**This salad also looks attractive made with a
mixture of coloured pasta rather than just plain.**

Serves 6
500g (1 lb) small pasta shapes of your choice
30g (1 oz) butter
1 red onion, chopped
1 cucumber, sliced
250g (8 oz) black olives
200g (7 oz) feta cheese, diced
freshly ground black pepper.

1 Cook pasta in boiling water in a large saucepan, following packet directions. Drain, set aside and keep warm.

2 Melt butter in a large frying pan and cook onion over a medium heat for 4-5 minutes or until soft. Add cooked onion, cucumber, olives, cheese and black pepper to taste to pasta and toss to combine. Serve immediately.

TAGLIATELLE SALAD

REALLY EASY!

As a lunch dish, this salad tossed in a Tomato and Basil Dressing needs only to be accompanied by crusty bread.

Serves 6
250g (8 oz) fresh spinach tagliatelle
250g (8 oz) fresh plain tagliatelle
2 courgettes, cut into matchsticks
1 small red pepper, sliced
1 small green pepper, sliced
200g (7 oz) green beans, cooked

Tomato And Basil Dressing
4 ripe tomatoes, skinned and roughly chopped
1 clove garlic, crushed
1 tablespoon olive oil
1 tablespoon red wine vinegar
2 tablespoons finely chopped fresh basil
1 tablespoon finely chopped fresh parsley
1 tablespoon snipped fresh chives
freshly ground black pepper

1 Cook both tagliatelle in boiling water in a large saucepan, following packet directions. Rinse under cold running water, drain and set aside to cool completely.

2 Place cold tagliatelle, courgettes, red and green peppers and beans in a large salad bowl.

3 To make dressing, place tomatoes, garlic, oil and vinegar in a food processor or blender and process until smooth. Stir in basil, parsley and chives and season to taste with black pepper. Spoon dressing over pasta and vegetables. Toss lightly to coat all ingredients with dressing.

WARM PASTA AND SALAMI SALAD

REALLY EASY!

Warm salads are perfect for winter days when only a light meal is required. This one is great accompanied by a salad of lettuce, olives and tomatoes.

Serves 4 as a light meal
250g (8 oz) large shell pasta
1 tablespoon olive oil
2 cloves garlic, crushed
60g (2 oz) pine kernels
125g (4 oz) salami, thinly sliced
1 tablespoon chopped fresh parsley

1 Cook pasta in boiling water in a large saucepan, following packet directions. Drain, set aside and keep warm.

2 Heat oil in a large frying pan and cook garlic and pine kernels, stirring constantly, over a medium heat for 1-2 minutes. Remove pan from heat and stir in salami and parsley. Add salami mixture to pasta and toss to combine. Serve warm.

MULTI-COLOURED PASTA

REALLY EASY!

V A mixture of cooked flavoured pasta tossed in a
French Dressing.

Serves 6 as an accompaniment
90g (3 oz) plain shell pasta
90g (3 oz) spinach shell pasta
90g (3 oz) tomato shell pasta
6 spring onions, chopped
1 small red pepper, diced
1 small green pepper, diced

French Dressing
2 tablespoons olive oil
4 tablespoons lemon juice
4 tablespoons white wine vinegar
¼ teaspoon dry mustard powder
½ teaspoon sugar
freshly ground black pepper

1 Cook plain, spinach and tomato pasta together in boiling water in a large saucepan, following packet directions. Drain, rinse under cold running water, then drain again and set aside to cool completely.

2 To make dressing, place oil, lemon juice, vinegar, mustard, sugar and black pepper to taste in a screw top jar and shake to combine.

3 Place pasta shells, spring onions and red and green peppers in a salad bowl. Pour dressing over and toss to combine.

WARM PASTA AND SALAMI SALAD • MULTI-COLOURED PASTA

CHICKEN GRAPE SALAD

REALLY EASY!

Moist chunks of chicken, green grapes and tarragon, tossed in a light dressing, combine the flavours of summer in this scrumptious salad.

Serves 6

250g (8 oz) small shell pasta
1.5 kg (3 lb) chicken, cooked and cooled
250g (8 oz) seedless green grapes
1 tablespoon chopped fresh tarragon
3 tablespoons mayonnaise
3 tablespoons natural yogurt
freshly ground black pepper

1 Cook pasta in boiling water in a large saucepan, following packet directions. Drain, rinse under cold running water, then drain again and set aside to cool completely.

2 Remove skin from chicken and discard. Strip flesh from chicken and chop. Place pasta, chicken, grapes and tarragon in a bowl and toss to combine.

3 Place mayonnaise, yogurt and black pepper to taste in a small bowl and mix to combine. Spoon over chicken mixture and toss to coat all ingredients. Serve at room temperature.

CHILLI AND BROAD BEAN SALAD

REALLY EASY!

Served with a tomato salad and garlic bread, this salad of pasta and beans with a hint of chilli makes a substantial main meal.

Serves 4
350g (12 oz) small shell pasta
1 tablespoon vegetable oil
250g (8 oz) shelled or frozen broad beans, skinned
1 teaspoon chilli paste (sambal oelek)
375 ml (12 fl oz) chicken stock
6 radishes, thinly sliced
2 tablespoons chopped fresh parsley
30g (1 oz) grated fresh Parmesan cheese

Garlic Dressing
60 ml (2 fl oz) olive oil
1 tablespoon cider vinegar
1 clove garlic, crushed
freshly ground black pepper

1 Cook pasta in boiling water in a large saucepan, following packet directions. Drain, rinse under cold running water, then drain again and set aside to cool completely.

2 Heat oil in a large frying pan and cook broad beans and chilli paste over a medium heat for 3 minutes. Stir in stock, bring to a gentle boil, cover and simmer for 10 minutes. Drain off any remaining liquid and set aside to cool.

3 To make dressing, place oil, vinegar, garlic and black pepper to taste in a screw top jar. Shake well to combine.

4 Place pasta, broad bean mixture, radishes, parsley and Parmesan cheese in a salad bowl. Pour dressing over and toss to combine.

CHICKEN PASTA SALAD

EASY!

Make this colourful salad of mixed pasta, vegetables and chicken in summer when fresh basil and oregano are at their best.

Serves 6

150g (5 oz) plain tagliatelle
150g (5 oz) spinach tagliatelle
150g (5 oz) tomato tagliatelle
2 tablespoons olive oil
2 red onions, cut into eighths
2 cloves garlic, crushed
500g (1 lb) chicken breast fillets, chopped
1 tablespoon finely chopped fresh oregano or 1 teaspoon dried oregano
1 tablespoon finely chopped fresh basil or 1 teaspoon dried basil
400g (14 oz) canned artichoke hearts, drained and halved
1 red pepper, cut into strips
90g (3 oz) green olives, drained
freshly ground black pepper

1 Cook plain, spinach and tomato tagliatelle together in boiling water in a large saucepan, following packet directions. Drain, rinse under cold running water, then drain again and set aside to cool completely.

2 Heat oil in a large frying pan and cook onions and garlic, stirring, over a medium heat for 2-3 minutes. Add chicken, oregano and basil and cook, stirring, for 10 minutes longer or until chicken is cooked. Remove pan from heat and set aside to cool completely. Place cooked chicken mixture, artichokes, red pepper, olives and tagliatelle in a large salad bowl. Season to taste with black pepper and toss to combine.

CHICKEN AND MANGO PASTA SALAD

REALLY EASY!

Leftover cooked turkey is a tasty alternative to chicken and when fresh mangoes are in season use these rather than the canned variety.

Serves 6
500g (1 lb) large shell pasta
1 cooked chicken, flesh cut into bite-sized pieces
200g (7 oz) canned water chestnuts, drained and sliced
400g (14 oz) canned mangoes, drained and sliced

Mango Chutney Dressing
250g (8 oz) mayonnaise
150g (5 oz) sweet mango chutney
2 spring onions, finely chopped
2 tablespoons chopped fresh coriander
freshly ground black pepper

1 Cook pasta in boiling water in a large saucepan, following packet directions. Drain, rinse under cold running water and drain again.

2 Place pasta, chicken, water chestnuts and mangoes in a bowl and toss to combine.

3 To make dressing, place mayonnaise, chutney, spring onions, coriander and black pepper to taste in a bowl and mix to combine. Spoon dressing over salad and mix to combine. Cover and chill until required.

147

TUNA AND ANCHOVY SALAD

REALLY EASY!

Made from store cupboard ingredients, this variation on a 'salade niçoise' brings together the tastes of the Mediterranean. Serve with herb bread and a salad of mixed lettuces for an easy and stylish lunch.

Serves 4 as a light meal
250g (8 oz) wholemeal pasta spirals
6 canned anchovies, drained
12 black olives
200g (7 oz) canned tuna, drained
1 tablespoon chopped fresh parsley
1 tablespoon snipped fresh chives
1 hard-boiled egg, cut in wedges

Mustard Dressing
1 teaspoon Dijon mustard
1 clove garlic, crushed
1 tablespoon white wine vinegar
60 ml (2 fl oz) olive oil
freshly ground black pepper

1 Cook pasta in boiling water in a large saucepan, following packet directions. Drain, rinse under cold running water, then drain again and set aside to cool completely.

2 Cut anchovies in half lengthwise. Wrap an anchovy strip around each olive. Place pasta, anchovy-wrapped olives, tuna, parsley and chives in a salad bowl.

3 To make dressing, place mustard, garlic, vinegar, oil and black pepper to taste in a screw top jar and shake well. Pour dressing over salad and toss to combine. Top with egg wedges.

35 # AVOCADO SALMON SALAD

REALLY EASY!

A pretty salad of pasta bows, avocado, smoked salmon, orange and dill.

Serves 4 as a light meal

350g (12 oz) pasta bows
1 large avocado, stoned, peeled and roughly chopped
1 teaspoon finely grated orange rind
2 tablespoons fresh orange juice
freshly ground black pepper
4 slices smoked salmon
4 sprigs fresh dill
1 orange, segmented

1 Cook pasta in boiling water in a large saucepan, following packet directions. Drain, rinse under cold running water, then drain again and set aside to cool completely.

2 Place avocado, orange rind, orange juice and black pepper to taste in a food processor or blender and process until smooth.

3 Place pasta in a bowl, top with avocado mixture and toss to combine. Roll salmon slices into cornets and fill with a dill sprig. Divide salad between four serving plates and top with salmon cornets and orange segments.

TUNA AND ANCHOVY SALAD • AVOCADO SALMON SALAD

PASTA WITH SPINACH TERRINE

**This loaf shaped terrine of pasta and vegetables
wrapped in prosciutto or ham is great for
a picnic or summer lunch.**

Serves 8
30g (1 oz) butter
1 large onion, finely chopped
2 cloves garlic, crushed
250g (8 oz) spinach fettucine
250g (8 oz) ricotta cheese
125g (4 oz) sour cream
4 tablespoons grated fresh Parmesan cheese
250g (8 oz) frozen spinach, thawed, drained and puréed
5 eggs, lightly beaten
45g (1½ oz) pine kernels, toasted and chopped
3 tablespoons coarsely chopped basil
freshly ground black pepper
12 slices prosciutto or ham

1 Melt butter in a frying pan and cook onion and garlic over a low heat for 4-5 minutes or until onion is soft. remove from heat and set aside.

2 Cook fettucine in boiling water in a large saucepan, following packet instructions. Drain, rinse under cold running water and set aside.

3 Preheat oven to 180C,350F,Gas 4. Place ricotta cheese, sour cream, reserved onion mixture, Parmesan cheese, spinach, eggs, pine kernels and basil in a food processor or blender and process until smooth. Season to taste with black pepper.

4 Chop fettucine roughly and mix with the cream mixture. Spoon into an oiled and lined 12 x 23 cm (4¾ x 9 inch) loaf tin. Cover with foil and place in a baking dish with enough hot water to come halfway up the sides of the tin. Bake for 35-40 minutes or until firm.

5 Cool terrine in tin for 10 minutes, then turn out and set aside to cool completely. Wrap prosciutto or ham slices around terrine to completely encase it. Serve cut into slices.

PASTA WITH SPINACH TERRINE

151

VEGETABLE PASTA SALAD

REALLY EASY!

 A delicious salad of pasta, broccoli, tomatoes, spring onions and olives with Red Wine Dressing.

Serves 4 as a meal or 8 as an accompaniment

500g (1 lb) small pasta shapes of your choice
250g (8 oz) broccoli, broken into florets
250g (8 oz) cherry tomatoes, halved
6 spring onions, cut into 2.5 cm (1 inch) lengths
12 black olives

Red Wine Dressing

2 tablespoons red wine vinegar
125 ml (4 fl oz) olive oil
2 tablespoons grated fresh Parmesan cheese
1 clove garlic, crushed
freshly ground black pepper

1 Cook pasta in boiling water in a large saucepan, following packet directions. Drain, rinse under cold running water, then drain again and set aside to cool completely.

2 Boil, steam or microwave broccoli for 2-3 minutes or until it just changes colour. Refresh under cold running water, drain, then dry on absorbent kitchen paper.

3 To make dressing, place vinegar, oil, Parmesan cheese, garlic and black pepper to taste in a screw top jar and shake to combine.

4 Place pasta, broccoli, tomatoes, spring onions and olives in a salad bowl. Pour dressing over and toss to combine.

SPIRAL PASTA SALAD

REALLY EASY!

[V] **A wonderful salad that combines all the best flavours of Italy. If you can, make it a day in advance so that the flavours have time to develop.**

Serves 4

500g (1 lb) spiral pasta
100g (3½ oz) sun-dried tomatoes, thinly sliced
100g (3½ oz) marinated or drained canned artichoke hearts, chopped
75g (2½ oz) sun-dried or roasted or drained bottled red peppers, chopped
125g (4 oz) marinated or drained canned black olives
12 small fresh basil leaves
60g (2 oz) Parmesan cheese shavings
1 tablespoon olive oil
3 tablespoons balsamic or red wine vinegar

1 Cook pasta in boiling water in a large saucepan, following packet directions. Drain, rinse under cold running water and set aside to cool completely.

2 Place pasta, sun-dried tomatoes, artichokes, red peppers, olives, basil, Parmesan cheese, oil and vinegar in a bowl and toss to combine. Cover and refrigerate for 2 hours or until ready to serve.

PASTA SALAD WITH ROASTED GARLIC

EASY!

The garlic can be roasted and the bacon and breadcrumb mixture cooked several hours in advance, leaving just the cooking of the pasta and the final assembly of the salad to do at the last minute.

Serves 6

20 cloves unpeeled garlic
8 rashers bacon, chopped
30g (1 oz) butter
125g (4 oz) breadcrumbs, made from stale bread
4 tablespoons chopped fresh mixed herb leaves
freshly ground black pepper
750g (1½ lb) spinach, tomato or plain spaghetti

1 Pre-heat oven to 180C,350F,Gas 4. Place unpeeled garlic cloves on a lightly greased baking tray and bake for 10-12 minutes or until soft and golden. Peel garlic and set aside.

2 Cook bacon in a frying pan over a medium heat for 4-5 minutes or until crisp. Drain on absorbent kitchen paper.

3 Melt butter in a clean frying pan, add breadcrumbs, herbs and black pepper to taste and cook, stirring, for 4-5 minutes or until breadcrumbs are golden.

4 Cook pasta in boiling water in a large saucepan, following packet directions. Drain well and place in a warm serving bowl. Add garlic, bacon and breadcrumb mixture, toss and serve immediately.

DESSERTS

Pasta for dessert does sound rather strange, but
it makes economic and imaginative puddings.
Lockshen Pudding is a traditional
Middle Eastern favourite.

LOCKSHEN PUDDING

EASY!

Egg vermicelli mixed with sultanas, mixed peel, almonds, cinnamon and eggs and baked in the oven.

Serves 4
250g (8 oz) egg vermicelli
60g (2 oz) unsalted butter, cut in small pieces
60g (2 oz) mixed candied peel
60g (2 oz) slivered almonds
60g (2 oz) sultanas
½ teaspoon ground cinnamon
60g (2 oz) caster sugar
2 eggs, beaten
150ml (¼ pint) thick double cream

1 Preheat oven to 180C, 350F, Gas 4. Cook the vermicelli according to packet instructions. Drain well and return to the dry pan with the butter, and stir until melted.

2 Add the mixed peel, 30g (1 oz) almonds, sultanas, cinnamon and sugar. Stir in the eggs and mix well. Put into a buttered ovenproof dish. Sprinkle over the remaining almonds and bake for 10-15 minutes or until set. Brown under a hot grill until crisp and serve with double cream.

APPLE LASAGNE

EASY!

**Layers of apples, lasagne and custard combine
to make this filling and satisfying dessert.**

Serves 4
750g (1½ lb) green apples, cored, peeled and sliced
30g (1 oz) butter
60g (2 oz) sugar
¼ teaspoon ground nutmeg
6 sheets lasagne, cooked
30g (1 oz) walnuts, finely chopped
2 tablespoons icing sugar, sieved

Egg Custard
300 ml (10 fl oz) milk
1 egg
1 egg yolk
1 tablespoon cornflour
1 tablespoon caster sugar

1 Place apples, butter, sugar and a little water in a saucepan and cook over a medium heat, stirring frequently, for 10 minutes or until apples are soft. Stir in nutmeg.

2 Preheat oven to 190C,375F,Gas 5. To make custard, heat milk in a saucepan and bring just to the boil. Place egg, egg yolk, cornflour and sugar in a bowl and whisk to combine. Whisk hot milk into egg mixture. Return custard to saucepan and cook, stirring constantly, over a low heat for 4-5 minutes or until custard thickens. Remove saucepan from heat.

3 Spread 2 tablespoons custard over base of a shallow ovenproof dish, then layer lasagne sheets and apples into dish, finishing with a layer of apple. Pour remaining custard over lasagne and sprinkle with walnuts. Bake for 25 minutes. Serve hot or warm, sprinkled with icing sugar.

APRICOT ORANGE PUDDING

EASY!

**A sauce of apricots and orange layered with
tagliatelle and walnuts and baked in the oven.**

Serves 6
125g (4 oz) dried apricots
250 ml (8 fl.oz) warm water
cinnamon stick
2 tablespoons fresh orange juice
2 teaspoons finely grated orange rind
90g (3 oz) soft brown sugar
2 teaspoons arrowroot blended with 2 teaspoons water
30g (1 oz) breadcrumbs, made from stale bread
125g (4 oz) tagliatelle
60g (2 oz) walnuts, ground
30g (1 oz) butter, melted

1 Place apricots in a bowl, pour warm water over and set
aside to soak for 1 hour. Drain apricots and reserve liquid.
Place apricots, 2 tablespoons reserved liquid, cinnamon stick,
orange juice, orange rind and 1 tablespoon brown sugar in
a saucepan. Bring to the boil, then reduce heat, cover and
simmer for 10-15 minutes or until apricots are tender.

2 Stir blended arrowroot into apricot mixture and cook
for 2-3 minutes longer or until mixture thickens. Remove
pan from heat and set aside to cool.

3 Preheat oven to 190C,375F,Gas 5. Cook tagliatelle in
boiling water in a large saucepan, following packet directions. Drain and set aside.

4 Coat a buttered 20 cm (8 inch) soufflé dish with breadcrumbs. Place one-third tagliatelle in base of soufflé dish
and top with half apricot mixture. Repeat layers, sprinkle
with walnuts and remaining sugar, and top with remaining tagliatelle. Pour butter over pudding and bake for 25
minutes. Turn onto a plate and cut into wedges to serve.

INDEX